TRAVEL G UZBEKISTAN 2024

All you need to know before your visit

Brent E. Ridgeway

Copyright © 2024 by Brent E. Ridgeway

All rights reserved. No part of this publication may be reproduced, distributed, or transmitted in any form or by any means, including photocopying, recording, or other electronic or mechanical methods, without the prior written permission of the publisher, except in the case of brief quotations embodied in critical reviews and certain other noncommercial uses permitted by copyright law. For permission requests, write to the publisher at the address below.

MY TRAVEL DIARY 7
CHAPTER ONE 10
  Territory and Inhabitants 10
    Overview of the Terrain 10
    Climate Overview 11
    Uzbek Population 13
    Historical Background 15
    Cultural Aspects 20
    Social Norms 21
  Customs and Traditions 26
    Cultural Celebrations 26
    Cultural Norms 29
    Interacting with Locals Traditionally 35
    Language Guide and Pronunciation Tips 36
    Non-Verbal Communication 40
    Presenting Gifts in Uzbekistan 42
    Photography Guidelines 43
    Dress Code when visiting Uzbekistan 44
CHAPTER THREE 46
  Key Travel Information 46
    Best Times to Visit 46
    Travel Formalities 47
    Transportation 48

Health Precautions 49

Safety Guidelines 50

Packing Essentials 51

Financial Planning 54

What to Buy and Eat 58

Food to Try 58

Things to Buy When Touring Uzbekistan 62

CHAPTER FOUR 66

Uzbekistan Cities 66

Tashkent 66

CHAPTER FIVE 91

The Fergana Valley of Uzbekistan 91

Namangan 91

Andijan 93

Fergana City 97

Margilan City 101

Kokand city 106

Samarkand and Dzhizak Provinces 111

Samarkand City 111

Dzhizak 115

CHAPTER SIX 119

Qashqa Darya and Surkhan Darya Provinces 119

Shakhrisabz 119

Boysun	124
Denau	126
Termez	130
CHAPTER SEVEN	136
Navoi Provinced	136
Karmana	141
Bukhara Province	145
Bukhara and Gijduvan	145
Khorezm Province	150
Urgench and Khiva	150
CONCLUSION	155

MY TRAVEL DIARY

Greetings, fellow adventurers! I recently embarked on an unforgettable journey to Uzbekistan and I'm thrilled to share my experiences with you. If you're in search of a unique travel destination, Uzbekistan should definitely be on your radar. Here's why.

Touchdown in Tashkent My adventure began in Tashkent, the bustling capital city. Tashkent is a lively metropolis, and the warmth and friendliness of the locals immediately struck me. The city offers a mix of modern and historical landmarks.

On my first day, I explored the city, visiting the impressive Khast Imam Complex and strolling through the vibrant Chorsu Bazaar. The bazaar was a feast for the senses with its array of colors and enticing smells.

Samarkand

A Journey Through History Next, I hopped on a train to Samarkand, one of the world's oldest cities. The train journey was comfortable and offered picturesque views of the countryside. Samarkand is famous for its stunning architecture. I visited the Registan, a large square flanked by three grand madrasahs (Islamic schools). The detailed designs and beautiful tiles left me spellbound. I also explored the Shah-i-Zinda, a street lined with mausoleums that felt like a walk through history. Every corner of Samarkand seemed to tell a story.

Bukhara

A City Steeped in History From Samarkand, I journeyed to Bukhara, a city steeped in history. Bukhara felt like a living museum. I meandered through its narrow streets, visited ancient mosques, and saw the formidable Ark Fortress. A memorable moment was visiting the Bolo Haouz Mosque, with its stunning wooden columns reflecting in the water. I also enjoyed unwinding in Lyabi-Hauz, a delightful square with a tranquil pond surrounded by cafes and restaurants.

Khiva

A Step Back in Time My last stop was Khiva, a city that seemed to have sprung from the pages of a fairy tale. Walking through Khiva felt like stepping back in time. The old town, Itchan Kala, is enclosed by high walls and filled with well-preserved buildings. I climbed to the top of the Kalta Minor Minaret for a panoramic view of the city. At night, the city transforms, with buildings beautifully lit up, creating a magical atmosphere.

The Cuisine

A Gastronomic Delight One of the highlights of my trip was the food. Uzbek cuisine is incredibly delicious! I tried plov, a hearty rice dish with meat and vegetables, which is the national dish. I also enjoyed samsa, pastries filled with meat or vegetables, and lagman, a flavorful noodle soup. Each meal was a new experience, and I loved trying different dishes at local eateries.

The People

The Heart of Uzbekistan What truly made my trip special were the people I met along the way. From friendly shopkeepers to kind locals, everyone was incredibly warm and welcoming. I even received an invitation to dine with a local family, which was a highlight of my trip. They shared their culture and traditions with me, making me feel like part of their family.

Why You Should Visit

Uzbekistan is a perfect blend of history, culture, and hospitality. It's a place where you can learn about the past while enjoying the present. Whether you're exploring ancient cities, savoring delicious food, or meeting friendly locals, there's something for everyone. If you're looking for a unique and unforgettable travel experience, I highly recommend visiting Uzbekistan. So pack your bags and get ready for an adventure of a lifetime. Uzbekistan is waiting for you!

CHAPTER ONE

Territory and Inhabitants

Overview of the Terrain

Uzbekistan, a Central Asian country, is home to parts of two significant mountain ranges, the Pamirs and the Tien Shan. The Kyzyl Kum Desert, located between the Amudarya (Oxus) and Syrdarya (Jaxartes) Rivers, is its most noticeable geographical aspect. Interestingly, Uzbekistan is one of only two countries worldwide that is doubly landlocked, meaning it is surrounded by other landlocked countries. With an area of 172,700 square miles (447,000 square kilometers), it is Central Asia's most populous country, with over thirty million residents. Only 10 percent of the land is irrigated, mainly in the river valleys and oases where most cities and the majority of the population reside. This leads to an uneven population distribution: the vast Karakalpak Autonomous Republic in the west makes up 37 percent of the country's area but only houses 5.7 percent of the population, while the fertile Ferghana Valley in the east, which covers just 5.1 percent of the land, is home to about 30 percent of the population. Mountains make up 23 percent of Uzbekistan's territory, with Babatag being the highest peak at 14,780 feet (4,668 meters) above sea level. Even though these mountains are not extremely high, generally below 6,000 feet (2,000 meters), they divide the country into distinct regions, especially in the south and east, making travel complex. The mountains almost surround the Ferghana Valley in the east and the smaller valleys in the south, forming natural barriers between cities like Jizzakh, Samarkand, and Shakhrisabz. The extensive Kyzyl Kum Desert is situated between Khoresm, an oasis area in the Amudarya delta, and the rest of the country. Historically, the rivers served as essential travel routes, initially by caravan and later by car and train. In 1924, Uzbekistan's borders were drawn to allocate land to new Soviet states. These borders were designed for administrative purposes, not to separate different peoples. When these countries gained independence in the early 1990s, the borders caused problems as they did not align with natural or ethnic divisions, disrupting internal unity and travel networks. The Tien Shan range isolates the Ferghana Valley from the rest of the country, with the only natural route passing through Tajikistan. The Hissar range separates the southern Surkhandarya province from the center. To improve travel, Uzbekistan built new roads and railways, linking Tashkent with Samarkand, the Ferghana Valley, and the southern regions, while also upgrading the Uzbek segment of the Transcaspian Railway. These improvements now allow travel from the oases to the desert through the mountains in a single journey.

Climate Overview

Uzbekistan is known for its distinctly continental climate, marked by hot, arid summers and variable winters.

Precipitation is scarce, primarily falling in late winter or spring. During the summer months of June and July, temperatures can soar up to 104°F (40°C), while winter temperatures average around 30°F (-1°C). It can occasionally drop as low as -4°F (-20°C) in January and February. Traditionally, periods of extreme temperatures, lasting for forty days, have become less consistent due to climate change. The seasons of spring and autumn are comparatively milder. The months of March and April bring unpredictable yet agreeable weather, with cold sunny days mixed with warmer cloudy ones. May and June are characterized by misty skies and rising temperatures. Following the intense summer heat, autumn ushers in cooler nights, although daytime temperatures can remain high. October is known for its clear skies and autumnal foliage, often swept away by the rains of November. Winter usually commences in December but has recently been shifting to January, introducing snow and freezing temperatures. The Aral Sea, previously the fourth-largest saltwater lake in the world, is shared between Kazakhstan and Uzbekistan. It was nourished by the Amudarya and Syrdarya Rivers, which transport meltwater from the Pamir and Tien Shan Mountains. However, the Soviet government's decision to divert these rivers for irrigation in the 1960s led to the Aral Sea's reduction. By 1990, irrigation initiatives had doubled the cultivated area, resulting in severe environmental problems such as salinization and pollution. In 1995, the countries surrounding the Aral Sea signed the Nukus Declaration to cooperate with the international community. Despite these efforts, the diminishing sea and salty dust storms have modified the regional climate. The smaller sea no longer tempers the cold northern winds or contributes moisture to mountain snowfall, decreasing the water supply to valleys. By the mid-2000s, the Aral Sea had divided into two smaller parts, with only the North Aral in Kazakhstan demonstrating some recovery. As the South Aral is primarily in Uzbekistan, the country plays a vital role in any initiatives to restore the Aral Basin. Uzbekistan's desert and mountainous regions experience more severe climates. Winters in the Kyzyl Kum Desert are chilly and windy, while summers are extremely hot. The hottest region is in the south, near the Afghanistan border. Global warming and the desiccation of the Aral Sea have led to shorter winters, decreased rainfall, and increased temperature variations.

Uzbek Population

Population and Culture s make up about 70 percent of the population, but Uzbekistan is a melting pot of cultures, with significant communities of Russians, Tajiks, Kazakhs, Karakalpaks, Koreans, Jews, Armenians, Tatars, and others. Despite the official policies that were based on the Soviet model of nation-building, Uzbeks are not a uniform ethnic group. They have diverse origins and were grouped under a single name in the 1920s and '30s. Contemporary Uzbeks are descendants of Turkic-Mongol nomads and other Turkic and Persian groups. Over the centuries, numerous Turkic-speaking nomadic tribes intermingled with Greeks, Chinese,

Arabs, and Mongols, integrating with the settled population who spoke ancient Persian dialects. This intermingling led to the emergence of different groups, dynasties, countries, and cultures over time, culminating in distinct modern nations in the early twentieth century. Presently, the government encourages a sense of Uzbek national identity to prevent ethnic divisions seen in other regions. Some groups have assimilated well. Many local Tajiks identify as Uzbek while preserving their Tajik language, likely due to their shared urban lifestyle, which has been a stronger bond than ethnic or language labels. The Karakalpaks, who live in the desert south of the Aral Sea, have a language and customs more similar to Kazakh than Uzbek. They had their own republic under the Soviet Union and continue to maintain autonomy within Uzbekistan. Ethnic Tajiks mainly reside in the historical cities of Samarkand and Bukhara. They differ from local Uzbeks primarily in language, although both groups widely speak Uzbek, Tajik, and Russian. Kazakhs and Kyrgyz, who were once nomadic, form substantial minorities in Uzbekistan, as do Iranians, Turkmen, and Uighurs. These groups are well assimilated with the Uzbek majority, preserving only some elements of their original cultures. A significant change in the ethnic composition of Central Asia took place from the 1850s to the 1880s when the Russian Empire colonized the region, leading to an influx of Russians. This included other Slavs like Ukrainians and Belarusians, and many Armenians, Germans, Jews, Poles, Tatars, Greeks, and others. They mainly settled in new cities. Although they now make up between 5 and 12 percent of the population, depending on how identity is interpreted, their influence on local culture has been significant. After gaining independence, many Russians and Russian-speakers of various ethnicities left Uzbekistan, altering its ethnic composition once again. Cities like Tashkent, Andijan, and Ferghana, which were only 30 to 50 percent Uzbek, are now almost entirely Uzbek. In 1990, 600,000 Germans lived in Uzbekistan; 95 percent have since left. Similarly, of the 260,000 Jews who lived in Uzbekistan in 1990, 90 percent have since left.

Historical Background

The Mongol invasion of Central Asia between 1219 and 1225 hastened the region's Turkification. The Mongol forces, composed of many Turkic horsemen, merged with the local Turkic- and Persian-speaking populations. The Mongols caused significant destruction to cities such as Bukhara and Samarkand and the entire Khoresm region. However, by the early 1300s, the Mongol empire began to fragment as various tribes and clans competed for power. From these conflicts, Timur (Tamerlane) rose as a formidable leader in the 1380s, establishing control over Transoxiana. He conquered Khoresm, Khorasan, Balkh, and regions near the Caspian Sea, eventually extending his control over Central Asia, Iran, Asia Minor, India, and the Caucasus. Timur became the most influential ruler in the Muslim world, defeating the Mamluks of Egypt and Syria, the emerging Ottoman Empire, and the declining Delhi Sultanate. He also launched an attack on Russia before dying during an invasion of China in 1405. Timur's legacy is multifaceted. While Central Asia prospered under his rule, other places like Baghdad, Damascus, and Delhi were sacked and devastated, with their populations significantly reduced. Nonetheless, Timur was the last great nomadic conqueror who brought a final period of prosperity to Transoxiana by attracting artisans and scholars to his capital, Samarkand. He supported science and the arts, and his grandson Ulugbek became one of the first great astronomers. During the Timurid dynasty, the Chaghatai dialect of Turkic evolved into a literary language, which was later adopted by new invaders from the north. The Uzbeks get their name from a group of Turkic-Mongol nomadic tribes who converted to Islam in the 14th century in southern Siberia. In the early 15th century, Abu al-Khayr Khan, a descendant of Genghis Khan, led them south to the steppe and semi-desert regions north of the Syrdarya River. By 1510, under Muhammad Shaybani Khan, they settled in the fertile lands of modern Uzbekistan. The Uzbeks displaced Timur's heirs from Samarkand and Herat (now in northwestern Afghanistan) and established new city-states. The most powerful of these was the khanate of Bukhara, which controlled the area between the Amudarya and the Syrdarya, as well as Tashkent, the fertile Ferghana Valley, and northern Afghanistan. The second Uzbek state, the khanate of Khiva, was founded in the Khoresm oasis in 1512. The Uzbeks transitioned from a nomadic lifestyle to urban life and agriculture. The initial century of Uzbek rule witnessed a cultural and artistic flourishing, but the

Shaybanid dynasty gradually declined, hastened by the end of Silk Road trade following the opening of sea routes to the east. In 1749, Iranian invaders took over Bukhara and Khiva, fracturing the weakened states. This led to the formation of the Emirate of Bukhara, including Samarkand, and the khanates of Khiva and Kokand, all of which were embroiled in perpetual internal conflicts until the Russians arrived. Tsarist Russia's interest in Central Asia grew in the 18th century, driven by concerns over British expansion from India, anger over Russian captives enslaved by local tribes, desires to control regional trade, and the need for a secure cotton supply. Additionally, Russia aimed to assert itself as an empire with its own eastern dominions. After several unsuccessful attempts, the Russians invaded the emirate of Bukhara in 1868 and brutally conquered the khanate of Khiva in 1873, making both protectorates with a quasi-independent status. In 1876, Kokand was annexed and made part of the Russian province of Turkestan, leading to an influx of Russian settlers. In the early years of Russian rule, the daily life of Central Asians remained largely unchanged. The Russians increased cotton production but otherwise minimally interfered with the locals. They built new towns adjacent to cities like Tashkent, Samarkand, Namangan, and Andijan but had little interaction with the indigenous population. Over time, Russian rule brought significant social and economic changes for many Uzbeks. A new, educated middle class emerged, and rural areas were increasingly affected by the focus on cotton production. The late 19th century saw the construction of the Transcaspian Railway, which brought more Russians to the region. In the 1910s, the Jadid reform movement, led by local intellectuals inspired by Turkish and Caucasian models, aimed to establish a new national community of Muslims in the region, free from conservative Islamic parochialism and colonial Russian rule. This movement fostered a growing awareness of national identities. Hopes for national autonomy or independence were sparked by an armed uprising against Tsarist conscription laws in 1916 and the subsequent Russian Revolutions of 1917. However, by 1921, it became clear that the Soviet regime had reunited the disintegrated Russian Empire, and new states were emerging. Some Jadidists and other loosely connected groups began the Basmachi Revolt against Soviet rule, which lasted for over a decade, while the majority of Jadidists, including their leaders, sided with the Soviets. In 1924, Soviet planners, local authorities, and Central Asian intellectuals defined the borders of the new Soviet Socialist Republics of Uzbekistan and Karakalpakstan based on dominant ethnic groups. In 1929, Tajikistan was split off from the south of Uzbekistan, causing lasting friction between Uzbeks, who viewed Tajiks as Persianized Uzbeks, and Tajiks, who were unhappy that the predominantly Tajik-speaking cities of Bukhara and Samarkand were given to the Uzbeks, whom the Tajiks saw as Turkic invaders from the north. Karakalpakstan was transferred to Uzbekistan in 1936 as an autonomous republic. By the beginning of World War II, the Soviet nationality-building program was firmly established. After the war, Soviet leaders managed to integrate diverse ethnic groups and subcultures into what would become Uzbek national culture. In the post-Stalin period, more Uzbeks began to join the Communist Party of Uzbekistan and assume government positions, albeit under Moscow's terms. Local Russians were gradually relegated to secondary roles or remained as respected but essentially powerless specialists providing technical expertise. As Uzbeks began to gain leading positions in society, they established informal networks based on regional and family connections and personal allegiances, which permeated official structures and provided support for the new generation of leaders. The liberalizing agenda of perestroika (reconstruction) launched by Soviet leader Mikhail Gorbachev in 1985 brought about social changes, including new opportunities for dissent and mounting economic challenges. Uzbeks expressed their grievances over the cotton monoculture, economic stagnation, Russian cultural domination, restrictions on religious and traditional life, and the lack of investment in industrial development to provide more job opportunities. Following bloody ethnic clashes in the Ferghana Valley between Uzbeks, Kyrgyz, and Meskhetian Turks (an ethnic subgroup deported from Georgia in 1944) in 1989 and 1990, Uzbek identity became more assertive. After the failure of the reactionary coup against Gorbachev in August 1991, Uzbekistan declared its independence from the USSR on September 1, 1991.

Present-Day Uzbekistan Although it has moved away from its communist past, the late President Islam Karimov, who once held the position of First Secretary of the Communist Party in Uzbekistan, retained stringent control over the independent nation. In many respects, Uzbekistan continues to bear a strong resemblance to the Soviet Union in both its public and private sectors. The presence of limited political opposition, a large bureaucratic class backed by an extensive police force, and numerous restrictions on human rights and civil liberties have ensured political stability, enabling Uzbekistan to weather several crises unscathed. Economic and demographic factors have led many young individuals, particularly from rural areas, to migrate to countries such as Russia, Kazakhstan, and Korea in pursuit of improved employment opportunities. This migration may have alleviated potential social tension, as it remains challenging for workers with fewer qualifications to secure well-paying jobs, especially in densely populated villages. Simultaneously, the relatively low cost of living, abundant local food supplies, and substantial financial resources have empowered the government to tackle some of the nation's issues. Progress has been made in areas such as the transportation network, rural housing, educational facilities, government services, and diversification of the economy. In summary, today's Uzbekistan is a country of contrasts—home to easy-going and welcoming individuals, yet governed by a rigid bureaucratic system. There is considerable scope for improvement in areas such as personal freedom, attractiveness for business, and transparency.

Cultural Aspects

Family The family unit is the bedrock of Uzbek society, with family values being maintained across all societal strata. Uzbek families usually have a patriarchal structure, a feature that, while evident to outsiders, is seldom questioned even by the women within these families. Traditionally, an Uzbek family is extended, encompassing several generations living around a communal courtyard in separate sections of a large house. With families often having five or six children and numerous relatives living in close proximity, Uzbek households are adaptable and supportive entities, well-integrated into a stable community. A key principle in family and societal organization is the hierarchy of age. Elderly members are revered, treated with respect, and cared for by their younger relatives, with the expectation that children will never put their parents in old age homes but will instead look after them within the family. Traditionally, Uzbek women are not expected to work outside the home. While this is often attributed to Islamic beliefs, it is more accurately a reflection of the patriarchal structure of society. In large families, women are typically engaged with household duties, and a woman working outside the home.

Social Norms
Respect for Elders

In Uzbek Families In Uzbek families, elders are held in high regard among younger members. It is a norm for younger individuals to address their parents, grandparents, and older people in general with respect. This respect is reflected in the Uzbek and Russian languages. Unlike English, which uses "brother" and "sister" generically, Uzbek has specific terms for older and younger siblings: "aka" for older brother, "uka" for younger brother, "opa" for older sister, and "singil" for younger sister. These terms are also used outside the family to show respect, similar to the honorific "-san" in Japanese. For example, Alisher-aka or Matluba-opa are respectful ways to address an older person. In formal settings, Uzbeks might use the Russian style of addressing elders by combining the first name with the patronymic, like Alisher Juraevich. In English, the second person pronoun "you" is neutral, but in Uzbek, "siz" (plural form) is used to show respect when addressing parents or elders, while "san" (singular form) is used for children or close friends and is considered rude otherwise. The rules in Russian are similar but more relaxed; children typically use "tee" (singular) with friends and parents, and "vee" (plural) for strangers and elders. Despite the traditional respect for elders, this does not always translate to authority in the workplace. Older individuals may have significant influence in private businesses or traditional crafts where their expertise is valued, but in more dynamic organizations, older employees are respected but may not always hold top positions. Some people feel that traditional respect for elders is declining in modern urban society, but overall, the core value remains: respect.

Attitudes toward Women

Attitudes toward women in Uzbekistan vary from liberal to traditional, depending on the community's expectations. Historically, Uzbek women were expected to stay home and care for children and relatives. This lifestyle, heavily influenced by Islamic norms, changed during the Soviet era, especially in urban areas where more liberal attitudes emerged. Legally, discrimination against women is banned in Uzbekistan, and women have more freedoms than in many Muslim-majority countries. They can pursue education, work in any profession, and hold any position. However, traditional attitudes often persist, influencing women's public standing and requiring them to navigate a complex social landscape. A female boss in Uzbekistan might be seen as strict at work but as a generous hostess in social settings. To an outsider, the life of a traditional Uzbek woman might seem restrictive. In conservative families, a girl's behavior is closely watched by her parents, who often arrange her marriage at a young age. After marriage, she is expected to be subordinate to her husband and mother-in-law. Many young women leave higher education to marry and face social pressure to have a child within the first year of marriage. Even in villages, it is now acceptable for women to work in roles related to household duties, such as teaching, nursing, or sewing. However, women are expected to return home immediately after work to prepare dinner for their families and risk damaging their reputations if seen alone in the evening. Women usually visit other families with their husbands and sit separately from men, attending special women-only events. Traditional women typically wear long dresses or skirts and have long hair, especially in conservative areas. While trousers have become more common for practical reasons, miniskirts and shorts are generally not accepted. Despite appearing subordinate, women in Uzbekistan have significant influence within their households. An Uzbek proverb, "The husband may be the head of the family, but the wife is the neck, which determines the direction where the head will look," captures this dynamic. Women manage their households and have substantial control over raising their children, instilling their values and ideals. They are the keepers of tradition, morals, and style, playing a crucial role even in the most conservative families. Gender relations in urban areas blend traditional attitudes with modern societal norms, such as equal education and employment rights, secular public life, and diverse cultural influences. Russian attitudes have significantly influenced urban gender dynamics, resulting in a unique blend of behaviors. The modern urban Uzbek woman skillfully navigates different social contexts, valuing independence and decision-making while maintaining her femininity. She avoids extreme feminism, seeking recognition and admiration without becoming a subservient housewife. Her ability to adapt to various social settings makes her versatile: even the most independent woman will be a caring mother and a gracious host. Women rarely live alone, and those who do might attract attention in the neighborhood. Russian and foreign women face fewer cultural restrictions but are not entirely free from traditional judgment. While smoking, wearing trousers, or socializing with men might be acceptable, excessive drinking or being out alone at night could be frowned upon. For female visitors to Uzbekistan, cultural sensitivity is key. While there's no expectation to dress traditionally or act like a housewife, it's wise to be aware of local customs and how certain behaviors may be interpreted.

Attitudes toward Homosexuality

Uzbekistan has laws against male homosexuality, but there are no known cases of people being convicted. By today's standards, Uzbekistan might be seen as homophobic, but the situation is complex. Historically, there were communities of teenage boys (bacha) who entertained guests, and this tradition is not completely forgotten. Additionally, because girls were traditionally unavailable for sexual activity, some boys experimented with each other. Therefore, it is public displays of homosexuality, rather than homosexuality itself, that people usually find objectionable. Female homosexuality is not illegal or particularly offensive, though the idea of same-sex families is still shocking to most people. Traveling with a same-gender partner is generally acceptable if the relationship looks like a typical friendship according to conservative norms.

Customs and Traditions
Cultural Celebrations
Nowruz

Nowruz, the traditional New Year in Central Asia, is a pre-Islamic festival celebrated on March 21 to welcome the onset of spring. Its roots can be traced back to Zoroastrianism. Preparations involve cleaning homes, washing carpets, adorning with flowers, and buying new clothes for visiting relatives and friends. All cleaning must be completed before the morning star rises on Nowruz day. The main event is preparing sumalak, a dish made from sprouting wheat grains, flour, and oil. Women from the community gather to take turns stirring it in a large pot. Once ready, the warm sumalak is shared with neighbors, relatives, and friends. Children enjoy Nowruz as they receive gifts of money and blessings from parents and older relatives.

Eid al-Fitr

Eid al-Fitr marks the end of Ramadan, the Islamic month of fasting. In Uzbekistan, it's referred to by various names such as Hayit Bayram, Uraza Bayram, Ruza Hayit, or Ramadan Hayit. The date varies each year based on the sighting of the new moon and usually occurs one day earlier in Uzbekistan than in many other Muslim countries. The celebrations last three days, during which people visit elders and neighbors and go to cemeteries to honor deceased relatives and clean their graves. Giving money to the poor is an important part of the celebration before performing the prayer that officially concludes the fasting month.

Eid al-Adha

Eid al-Adha, or Kurban Bayram, is observed sixty-eight days after Eid al-Fitr. It commemorates Abraham's willingness to sacrifice his son in obedience to God. The main ritual involves the sacrifice of an animal, typically a sheep. The meat is divided into three parts: one-third is kept by the family, another third is distributed to relatives, friends, and neighbors, and the final third is given to the poor and needy.

Easter Easter, celebrated by the Orthodox Church, usually falls in April or May, typically a week after Western Easter. On the Saturday evening before Easter Sunday, people gather at Orthodox churches a few hours before midnight. Many attendees are not regular churchgoers, and some Muslims also join the celebration. People bring boiled and decorated eggs and special cakes to be blessed by priests. A solemn procession around the church commemorates the Resurrection of Christ, followed by a service inside the church. On Easter Sunday morning, people visit friends and relatives, exchanging eggs, cakes, and kisses while greeting each other with "Christ has risen!" For many Russians, this is their main religious observance of the year.

Ex-Soviet Holidays After gaining independence, Uzbekistan removed nearly all Soviet holidays from public life. The first to go were the Day of the Revolution (November 7) and

International Labor Day (May 1). Victory Day is still celebrated on May 9 but was renamed the Day of Memory and Remembrance in 1999 to honor all Uzbek soldiers who died in various conflicts. Constitution Day and the Day of the Defenders of the Motherland, previously observed on December 5 and February 23, were moved to December 8 and January 14, respectively. March 8, International Women's Day, remains an important holiday. Women typically receive gifts on this day, especially at work. In the absence of a similar festival for men, Defenders' Day served as an occasion to give men presents. While some people continue to celebrate it on February 23, others have adopted January 14 for this purpose. Among former Soviet holidays, the most popular is New Year's Day on January 1. This holiday has evolved from Russian New Year and Christmas traditions, including a New Year tree topped with a star, Grandfather Frost, and the Snow Maiden. The celebration also includes a televised address by the president, performances by singers and dance troupes, the clock striking twelve, and traditional snacks. In Uzbekistan, these customs have been slightly modified: the red star is replaced by an eight-pointed star or a bird, and Grandfather Frost's red gown is now dark blue. The New Year's celebration highlights the blend of traditions in Uzbekistan's urban culture.

Other Holidays

Halloween and Valentine's Day have become popular among young people in larger cities due to global influences, though they are controversial. In the 2010s, authorities launched public campaigns against these holidays, calling them inappropriate for local culture. Valentine's Day was criticized for undermining Islamic values of pure love, and Halloween was dismissed as "foreign" and "unpopular," leading to bans on Halloween parties in restaurants and nightclubs. Despite this, many young people continue to celebrate these holidays in private settings.

Cultural Norms

In Uzbekistan, tradition is a fundamental part of everyday life, influencing how people dress, eat, and interact, as well as their views on work, rules, and authority. This concept aligns with other enduring terms like "national," "mentality," "character," "ancestors," and "our people." While customs and traditions are evidently evolving, many believe there is an essence of "true" Uzbek traditions that have always existed but were obscured by political and historical events. Many people think these authentic traditions are now resurfacing. However, everyday life in Uzbekistan demonstrates that family, community, work, religion, culture, and national customs are constantly changing and more fragile than they appear. Despite this, people cling to customs from their childhood, believing they connect them to their ancestors and the country's rich history and culture. This mindset is prevalent among Uzbeks and less so among

Russian communities. Generally, people cherish their traditions and actively engage in ethnic rituals that link them to their native culture, even as modern influences grow stronger.

The most traditional Uzbek ceremonies are tied to significant life events—birth, marriage, and death. These events involve community members, including relatives, neighbors, colleagues, and local authorities, as well as many honored guests. Rooted in both pre-Islamic and Islamic practices, these ceremonies have been shaped by a century of secular influences and external cultural impacts, first from Russia and now from Europe, Turkey, Arabia, and China. For instance, Chinese fabrics with distinctive patterns and colors are now used to make traditional Uzbek clothing. Similarly, Uzbek men often buy pajamas from the UAE and wear plastic bathroom slippers outdoors, reflecting cultural borrowing.

Guidebooks and travel blogs on Uzbekistan highlight the role of traditional rituals and customs in everyday life, emphasizing their distinctiveness to foreign visitors. This focus on rituals is often due to the hospitality extended to foreigners, who may attend many ceremonial feasts and find them exotic.

However, it is the underlying values and attitudes of the Uzbek people that truly define the local culture. One of the most traditional Uzbek ceremonies is Beshik-tuy, the wooden cradle festival, which celebrates placing a newborn baby in a cradle for the first time. Usually held on the seventh, ninth, or eleventh day after the baby's birth, the ceremony varies by region and family income. Relatives, mostly from the mother's side, bring the cradle, tablecloth, cakes, sweets, and toys, along with gifts for the baby's parents and grandparents. These items are transported to the family house with much fanfare, including local wind instruments.

Traditionally, the baby's grandfather receives the cradle and passes it to his son, who then gives it to the baby's mother. In some villages, white flour is daubed on faces to signify pure thoughts, a practice still used in other ceremonies. While guests enjoy a lavish table of food and music, older women teach the young mother how to swaddle and prepare the cradle. At the end of the ceremony, guests visit the baby and place gifts, money, or sweets on the tablecloth spread in front of the cradle. In contrast, in Russian and other Christian communities, the birth of a baby is a private affair, with only close relatives involved until the baby is forty days old.

After this period, relatives and friends may celebrate, and the mother can take the baby out. These rules are becoming more relaxed over time. For Koreans, the most significant celebration of a baby is not the birth itself, but milestones like the twenty-first and hundredth days, with the main ceremony on the baby's first birthday. The day starts with family rituals, traditional costumes, and a custom where the baby "chooses its destiny" by picking an object from several laid out in front of it. The celebration often concludes with a lavish supper, loud music, dancing, and alcohol in a restaurant with relatives, friends, and colleagues.

Names in Uzbekistan provide insights into a person's ethnic, social, and family background. Officially, names follow the Soviet pattern of surname, first name, and patronymic, but this system has diversified since the end of the USSR. Uzbek names reflect the country's rich history, with most originating from Arabic, Persian, or Turkic roots. In recent years, it has become popular to extend short Arabic names with prestigious prefixes or suffixes and to remove Russian endings from surnames. For instance, Akbar Akhmedov might become Shoakbarkhon Mirakhmad. Patronymic endings have also been changed from Russian to Uzbek forms.

Some Uzbek names reflect family history or circumstances, such as names given to twins or names that signify a wish for boys. Children are never named after a living relative. Tajik names are similar, except for distinctly Turkic ones. Russians have retained their traditional names, though the range of acceptable first names has narrowed. Armenian surnames end with -yan or -yantz, and Georgian with -dze, -iani, -atia, or -shvili. Tartars share some surnames with Uzbeks and Russians, and their names often reflect traditional Muslim names or European adaptations. Koreans have a limited choice of surnames and often use Russian first names. In mixed families, children may have names reflecting multiple traditions.

Circumcision, known as Khantakilish or Sunnat-tuy, is a significant ceremony required by Islam. Traditionally performed on young boys, there is a trend toward circumcising infants in urban families. Sunnat-tuy is a major event involving extensive preparations and community participation. The ceremony begins with prayers and includes token gifts for children. The boy, dressed in bright clothes, is traditionally brought to the ceremony riding a colt, symbolizing his transition to manhood. However, this practice is declining in cities. The circumcision itself is performed by a local medicine man, though laser circumcision is becoming popular. The ceremony ends with a lavish dinner, often featuring the traditional dish plov.

Weddings are the most important and varied traditional rituals in Uzbek culture, reflecting regional, class, and stylistic differences. They combine traditional elements with modern aspirations and include both religious and civil ceremonies. The official engagement, fatiha-tuy, involves a formal ceremony at the bride's house, followed by negotiations and planning for the wedding. The wedding day features a series of rituals, including the eating of wedding plov and the formal marriage ceremonies. The bride's farewell to her family and transition to the groom's house is a significant part of the wedding. The celebration often ends with a restaurant party, which has become a key aspect of modern weddings. Russian weddings are less elaborate than Uzbek ones but are lively and entertaining. The official registration takes place at the Civic Registry, and some couples also have a church ceremony. After the official part, the couple and their guests tour the city for photos and champagne before the main reception, which includes music, dancing, toasts, and food. Many urban cultures have adopted elements of the Russian wedding. An interesting Uzbek ceremony is the "morning plov," held on one of the wedding days or as a commemorative ritual. It takes place early in the morning, so participants can attend before work. The ceremony involves preparing plov and inviting guests to share the meal, reinforcing social ties and commitments.

Traditionally, Muslims in Uzbekistan did not celebrate birthdays, but this custom has been adopted from the Russians and is now widely practiced across different ethnic communities. Birthdays are celebrated with family, friends, and colleagues, involving special cakes and gifts. Important birthdays include milestones like sixteen, eighteen, twenty-five, fifty, and sixty-three, the latter marking the age of Prophet Muhammad's death.

Funerals in Uzbekistan are highly traditional. Muslims follow Islamic practices with local features, including burying the deceased on the day of death and holding commemoration ceremonies. Russian funerals are more complex, following Eastern Orthodox traditions. Armenian funerals are particularly solemn, with men refraining from shaving for forty days. Cemeteries feature elaborate tombstones reflecting various cultural traditions.

Superstitions play a significant role in everyday life in Uzbekistan, influencing both personal and official practices. Common Uzbek superstitions include keeping bread "face up," buying items in pairs, and using charms like blue beads or old shoes to ward off evil spirits. Such beliefs are integrated into the diverse cultural fabric of the country.

Interacting with Locals Traditionally

Socializing in Uzbekistan primarily takes place at home, a practice that continues to be prevalent in many areas. However, in larger cities, meeting in cafés and restaurants has become increasingly popular. These dining venues typically fall into two categories: Uzbek and others. Uzbek restaurants offer traditional dishes at reasonable prices and cater to large gatherings in settings that are simple yet lively. Most public ceremonies that are not held at home now occur in these restaurants, some of which are dedicated venues for large parties (tuy-hona). Other dining options include local fast-food joints, modest beer spots, stylish bars, and high-end themed restaurants serving a variety of international cuisines. Many of these places stay open late and are popular with groups looking to enjoy themselves. It's advisable to visit these places with a friend who is familiar with the local scene, as ownership, styles, and clientele can change frequently. In Tashkent and tourist cities like Samarkand, Bukhara, and Khiva, there are restaurants and bars that cater to tourists and expatriates. While these may not offer the most authentic experiences, they provide a comfortable setting for cross-cultural interactions. Nightclubs are rare and are viewed by locals as "small pockets of freedom," where activities can get quite lively. The same applies to semi-underground bars frequented by local artists and hipsters, which offer an interesting, though not always polished, cultural experience.

Language Guide and Pronunciation Tips

Introduction to Uzbek Language

Uzbek, the national language of Uzbekistan, is part of the Turkic language family and is spoken by the majority of the population. While Russian is also widely spoken and understood, particularly in urban areas and among the older generation, learning some basic Uzbek phrases can greatly enrich your travel experience. This guide will assist you with essential words and phrases, their pronunciations, and some tips for effective communication.

Pronunciation Guide

Uzbek pronunciation can be a challenge for beginners, but with practice, you can master it. Here are some key points to remember:

- Vowels: Uzbek vowels are generally pronounced as follows:
  - A: as in "father"
  - E: as in "bed"

- I: as in "machine"
- O: as in "pot"
- U: as in "rude"
- Ö: as in "bird" (similar to German)
- Ü: as in "müde" (similar to French "lune")

- **Consonants**: Most consonants are pronounced as in English, but there are a few differences:
  - C: pronounced like "ts" in "cats"
  - G: always hard, as in "go"
  - Q: a deeper "k" sound, produced from the back of the throat
  - X: similar to the "kh" sound in "Bach" or Arabic "خ"

Basic Phrases and Their Pronunciations

Here are some essential phrases to help you get started:

1. Greetings and Basic Expressions

- Hello: Salom (sah-LOHM)
- How are you?: Qalay siz? (kah-LAI sehz)
- I am fine, thank you: Yaxshi, rahmat (yahk-SHI, rah-MAHT)
- Please: Iltimos (eel-tee-MOHS)
- Thank you: Rahmat (rah-MAHT)
- Yes: Ha (hah)
- No: Yo'q (yohk)

2. Useful Phrases for Travelers

- Excuse me / Sorry: Kechirasiz (keh-chee-RAH-sehz)
- Do you speak English?: Siz inglizcha gapirasizmi? (sehz in-GLEEZ-chah gah-pee-rah-SEEZ-mee)
- How much is this?: Bu qancha turadi? (boo KAHN-chah too-RAH-dee)
- Where is the bathroom?: Hojatxona qayerda? (HOH-jaht-khoh-NAH kah-YEHR-dah)
- Help!: Yordam bering! (yor-DAHM BEH-ring)

Numbers

- One: Bir (beer)
- Two: Ikki (ee-kee)
- Three: Uch (ooch)
- Four: To'rt (toh-rt)
- Five: Besh (besh)
- Six: Olti (ohl-tee)
- Seven: Yetti (yet-tee)
- Eight: Sakkiz (sak-KEEZ)
- Nine: To'qqiz (tohk-KEEZ)
- Ten: O'n (ohn)

Days of the Week

- Monday: Dushanba (doo-SHAHN-bah)
- Tuesday: Seshanba (seh-SHAHN-bah)
- Wednesday: Chorshanba (chor-SHAHN-bah)
- Thursday: Payshanba (pah-ee-SHAHN-bah)
- Friday: Juma (joo-MAH)

- Saturday: Shanba (shahn-BAH)
- Sunday: Yakshanba (yak-SHAHN-bah)

Tips for Effective Communication

- **Speak Slowly and Clearly:** This helps avoid misunderstandings and makes it easier for locals to understand you.
- **Use Gestures:** Non-verbal communication can bridge language gaps.
- **Be Polite:** Using polite phrases like "please" and "thank you" goes a long way in making a good impression.
- **Learn Basic Numbers:** Knowing numbers can be particularly useful for shopping and bargaining.
- **Practice Common Phrases:** Repetition will help you become more comfortable with the sounds and rhythms of Uzbek.

Cultural Considerations

Understanding cultural norms is crucial for effective communication. Here are a few pointers:

- **Greeting Etiquette:** Uzbeks typically greet each other with a handshake accompanied by a slight bow and placing the left hand over the heart.
- **Respect for Elders:** Show respect by addressing elders and using polite language.
- **Hospitality:** Uzbeks are known for their hospitality. Accepting offers of tea or food is considered polite.

Non-Verbal Communication

In Uzbekistan, most locals prefer to converse while standing close to each other, typically less than three feet (one meter) apart. Physical contact is common among individuals of the same gender, such as women touching each other's arms or sitting closely, and men draping their arms around each other's shoulders, particularly at social events. Hugging is a common practice, and older individuals are generally more physically expressive than the younger generation. It's not uncommon for friends of the same gender to hold hands in public.

However, interactions between men and women involve more physical distance, although this is less noticeable in multicultural settings. At traditional Uzbek gatherings, men and women often sit separately, and even at mixed or multicultural events, men and women may form separate groups to discuss topics like clothing and relationships for women, and sports and politics for men. Direct eye contact is typical among peers of the same gender but is less common when interacting with the opposite sex, older people, or superiors.

Uzbek people often observe their surroundings and will openly stare at anything unusual or interesting. For instance, traffic accidents attract onlookers who gather to watch. In less traditional settings, such as on the underground train, Uzbeks behave similarly to passengers in New York or

London, staring into space, reading, or using their cell phones.

In office environments, personal space is not as clearly divided into private and public areas as in the West. Shared spaces are common, and items like tea, coffee, and sugar are communal, with everyone contributing to their purchase. While personal mugs are used daily, there is typically a large tea set for corporate celebrations.

Gestures

Young men in Uzbekistan tend to use more active gestures, while women and older men are more reserved. Though not as expressive as Italians or Latin Americans, Uzbeks still use various gestures often. Here are some common ones:

- **Washing your face with both hands:** This gesture, taken from a Muslim prayer, marks the end or beginning of something, like a meal, journey, or exam.

- **Pressing the right hand to the chest:** This is a sign of respect or apology and is also used as a greeting or farewell.

- **Pressing the left hand to the chest while using the right hand:** This shows extra respect, especially when pointing at something, shaking hands, or offering tea.

- **Rubbing the index finger and thumb together:** This means money or price.

- **Tapping the right temple with the index finger:** This indicates that someone is foolish or stupid.

- **Flicking a finger at one's neck:** This can either be an invitation to drink or a sign that someone is drunk.

Presenting Gifts in Uzbekistan

The tradition of gift-giving is significant and forms an integral part of their culture. When you are invited to someone's home, it's customary to bring a small token of appreciation. Suitable gifts include sweets, baked goods, or fruit, which are always appreciated by the host. It's also a good idea to consider bringing something from your own country, as it adds a personal touch and can lead to interesting conversations. When offering your gift, use both hands or the right hand, as this demonstrates respect and sincerity. Refrain from giving alcohol unless you are certain that the recipients consume it, as many Uzbeks are Muslim and may abstain from alcohol. If you are invited to a special occasion, such as a wedding or a birthday, more substantial gifts like kitchenware, home decorations, or even money are appropriate. Always wrap your gifts nicely, as the presentation is considered part of the gesture. Gifts are typically given and received with genuine gratitude. However, it is common for the recipient not to open the gift immediately in front of the giver. This custom is rooted in modesty and the desire not to appear greedy. Instead, the gift will be set aside to be opened later, and the recipient will thank you sincerely.

Photography Guidelines

When taking photographs in Uzbekistan, it's essential to be mindful of cultural norms and local sensitivities. Always ask for permission before photographing people, especially in rural areas where traditional values are more prevalent. A simple gesture towards your camera, accompanied by a smile, usually suffices to ask for consent. If the person agrees, a polite "thank you" in Uzbek (rahmat) will be appreciated. Be cautious when photographing religious sites and ceremonies. Some places, especially inside mosques or during prayer times, may have restrictions on photography. Look for signs or ask a local for guidance to avoid offending anyone. Similarly, avoid taking photos of military installations, government buildings, and other sensitive areas, as this can lead to misunderstandings or legal issues. When photographing markets, bustling streets, and everyday scenes, try to be discreet. Avoid being intrusive, and respect people's privacy. Capturing candid moments can be rewarding, but it's crucial to do so respectfully. In tourist areas, like Samarkand, Bukhara, and Khiva, people are generally more accustomed to visitors with cameras, and you will find many beautiful and photogenic spots. Nevertheless, showing respect and politeness goes a long way in ensuring a positive experience. If you promise to send someone a photo you've taken of them, make sure to follow through, as this small act of kindness can leave a lasting positive impression.

Dress Code when visiting Uzbekistan

It is important to dress appropriately to show respect for the local culture and traditions. While urban areas like Tashkent are more relaxed, with people wearing modern, Western-style clothing, it's still wise to dress conservatively. In rural areas and smaller towns, traditional values are stronger, and modesty in clothing is highly appreciated. For men, wearing long pants and shirts with sleeves is a good rule of thumb. Shorts are not commonly worn by local men and may attract unwanted attention. Lightweight, breathable fabrics are ideal for the hot summer months, while layering is useful for the cooler seasons. For women, modesty is key. Opt for skirts or dresses that fall below the knee or long pants, and avoid sleeveless tops. A scarf is useful for visiting religious sites, where covering your head might be required. While it's not mandatory to wear traditional clothing, incorporating elements such as a tunic or shawl can be a respectful nod to local customs. Footwear should be practical and comfortable, especially since you might be walking on uneven surfaces or visiting historical sites. In religious places, you might be asked to remove your shoes, so wearing easily removable footwear can be convenient. In general, bright and flashy clothing should be avoided, as it might be seen as inappropriate. Neutral or muted colors are preferable and help you blend in more with the local populace. Accessories should also be modest; expensive jewelry or showy items can be seen as ostentatious. During the hot summer months, staying cool while remaining modest can be a challenge. Lightweight, loose-fitting clothes made from natural fibers like cotton or linen are excellent choices. They keep you comfortable and adhere to the local standards of modesty. When attending special events or family gatherings, dressing up a bit more is a sign of respect. Men might wear a nice shirt and trousers, while women could opt for a dress or a traditional outfit. Always consider the nature of the event and dress accordingly.

CHAPTER THREE

Key Travel Information

Best Times to Visit

Spring (March to June): Spring comes early in Uzbekistan, with apricot trees beginning to bloom as early as March. The weather during this season is warm and relatively dry, with temperatures ranging from 14°C (57°F) to 30°C (86°F). It's a great time to explore the historical cities of Samarkand, Bukhara, and Khiva, enjoy mountain retreats, or immerse yourself in the art and culture of Tashkent. However, spring is also the busiest and rainiest season, so it's advisable to plan your travel and accommodation in advance.

Autumn (September to early November): Autumn brings mild and pleasant weather, with daytime temperatures typically between 21°C (70°F) and 30°C (86°F). It's a wonderful season for fruit lovers, as Uzbekistan's famous melons and watermelons are ripe for the picking. A highlight of autumn is visiting the Fergana Valley during harvest time, especially around Margilan, known for its extensive grape growers' houses.

Winter (December to January): Despite being known for its continental climate, Uzbekistan surprises winter sports enthusiasts with quality snow and improving infrastructure. The opening of the Amirsoy mountain resort in 2019, conveniently located near Tashkent, has positioned Uzbekistan as Central Asia's emerging high-end skiing destination. Keep in mind that Uzbekistan experiences extreme weather due to its continental climate, so be prepared for varying conditions throughout the year.

Travel Formalities

Visa Information: Travelers from countries like Azerbaijan, Armenia, Belarus, Georgia, Kazakhstan, Kyrgyzstan, Moldova, Russia, or Ukraine enjoy visa-free entry. Additionally, citizens of nations such as Australia, Austria, Brazil, Germany, Finland, France, Japan, and others can visit Uzbekistan for up to 30 days without a visa. However, if you're not from these countries, you'll need to obtain a visa. This can be done through the Uzbekistan e-Visa System online or at an Uzbek Embassy or Consulate. The e-Visa typically takes three days to process, and you'll receive it via email.

Entry Regulations: Ensure your passport remains valid for at least three months beyond your intended stay. There are no specific COVID-19 testing or vaccination requirements for entry into Uzbekistan. However, it's mandatory to register with the local district OVIR (Department of Foreign Travel and Exit) within three days of arrival. Hotels typically handle this registration on behalf of guests, while those staying in private accommodations should ensure their host completes the registration process.

Transportation

Arriving in Uzbekistan:

- **By Air:** The most convenient way to reach Uzbekistan is by air. The primary international airport is located in Tashkent (TAS), although there's also one in Samarkand (SKD).

- **By Land:** For those traveling overland, entry into Uzbekistan is possible by car or bus from neighboring countries.

Getting Around Uzbekistan:

- **By Train:** Uzbekistan boasts a well-established railway network. Modern, high-speed trains, reminiscent of airplane seating, operate from Tashkent to Samarkand and further to Bukhara. Additionally, Russian-style sleeper trains offer an atmospheric overnight travel experience. It's advisable to book train tickets well in advance, preferably up to 45 days, either online or through the Uzbekistan Railways app.

- **By Road:** Uzbekistan features an extensive road network, although infrastructure conditions vary, particularly outside of Tashkent. Travelers can opt for cars, buses, or taxis. While taxis are cost-effective, it's essential to agree on the fare beforehand.

- **By Subway:** Tashkent is home to Central Asia's first underground transport system, the subway.

- **By Air:** Domestic flights connect the major cities within the country, offering another convenient mode of transportation.

Health Precautions

Vaccinations: Prior to your travel, make sure you are up-to-date on all routine vaccinations. This includes immunizations for diseases such as Chickenpox, Diphtheria-Tetanus-Pertussis, Flu, Measles-Mumps-Rubella (MMR), Polio, and Shingles. It's also essential for all eligible travelers to have received their COVID-19 vaccines. Specifically for Uzbekistan, the CDC recommends getting vaccinated against Hepatitis A and Hepatitis B. Hepatitis A can be contracted through contaminated food or water, irrespective of where you eat or stay. Hepatitis B is transmitted through sexual contact, contaminated needles, and blood products.

Food and Water Safety: To maintain good health, only consume bottled or boiled water. Be mindful of the food and water quality, as standards can differ by location. Refrain from consuming raw or undercooked meat and fish.

Prevent Bug Bites: Mosquitoes, ticks, and fleas in Uzbekistan can carry diseases. Use insect repellent, wear long sleeves and pants, and opt for accommodations with air conditioning or proper window and door screens.

Stay Safe Outdoors: If you plan to engage in outdoor activities, take precautions to stay healthy. Avoid swimming in freshwater to minimize the risk of water-borne diseases.

Avoid Animal Contact: Direct contact with animals can spread diseases. If you will be spending significant time outdoors in rural areas, consider getting a pre-exposure rabies vaccination.

Safety Guidelines

- **Stay Aware:** Always be alert of your surroundings and keep an eye on your belongings, especially in crowded places.

- **Avoid Night Travel:** Avoid walking alone at night, particularly in areas you are not familiar with.

- **Public Transport:** Exercise caution when using public transportation, especially during nighttime.

- **Secure Your Valuables:** Keep your valuables, including your passport and money, in a safe and secure place.

- **Avoid Demonstrations:** Stay away from political demonstrations and public gatherings to avoid potential risks.

- **Respect Local Customs:** Be mindful and respectful of local customs and traditions, particularly when visiting religious sites.

Packing Essentials

Uzbekistan's diverse landscapes and rich cultural experiences call for careful packing. Here's a comprehensive guide to ensure you have everything needed for a smooth and enjoyable trip:

Clothing:

1. **Climate Considerations:** Uzbekistan has a continental climate with hot summers and cold winters. Pack according to the season you'll be visiting.

2. **Layering:** Bring a mix of light, breathable clothes for warm days, and some warmer layers like sweaters or a light jacket for cooler evenings and temperature drops, especially in spring and autumn.

3. **Long Pants and Sleeved Shirts:** Wear long pants and shirts with sleeves, especially when visiting religious sites, to respect local customs.

4. **Comfortable Shoes:** Pack sturdy walking shoes or boots for exploring historical sites and uneven terrain. Sandals are great for hot days but may not be suitable for all activities.

5. **Swimwear:** If you plan to stay in hotels with pools or visit swimmable lakes, pack a swimsuit and a beach towel.

6. **Headwear:** A hat and sunglasses are essential for sun protection, particularly during summer.

7. **Warm Accessories:** Depending on the season, bring a scarf, gloves, and a warm hat for chilly evenings or winter travel.

Essentials:

1. Passport and Visa: Ensure your passport is valid for at least six months and obtain the necessary visa for Uzbekistan before your trip.

2. **Travel Insurance:** Get travel insurance to protect against unexpected medical emergencies or travel disruptions.

3. **Photocopies:** Make copies of your passport and visa for safekeeping, and consider keeping digital copies as well.

4. **Cash:** Carry Uzbek som (UZS) in small denominations for everyday purchases, taxis, and places where cards aren't accepted.

5. **Debit/Credit Cards:** Inform your bank of your travel plans to avoid card issues. Credit cards are increasingly accepted in major cities, but don't rely solely on them.

6. **First-Aid Kit:** Pack basic medications like pain relievers, anti-diarrheal medicine, and bandages.

7. **Personal Toiletries:** Bring your usual toiletries, including sunscreen with SPF 30 or higher, lip balm, and hand sanitizer.

Travel Comfort and Convenience:

1. Daypack: A comfortable daypack is essential for carrying daily necessities.

2. Water Bottle: Stay hydrated, especially in hot weather. Use a reusable water bottle to reduce plastic waste.

3. Universal Adapter: Ensure you can charge your devices by packing a universal adapter.

4. Electronics: Bring your phone, camera, chargers, and consider a portable power bank for extended outings.

5. Entertainment: Download movies, audiobooks, or podcasts for long journeys or downtime.

6. Guidebook and Maps: A guidebook or travel app can provide valuable information, and offline maps are useful for navigating unfamiliar areas.

7. Eye Mask, Earplugs, and Travel Pillow: These items can improve your comfort during travel.

Remember:

1. Adapt the List: Customize this list based on your itinerary, interests, and the time of year you'll be visiting.

2. Luggage Restrictions: Check luggage restrictions for your airline to avoid excess baggage fees.

3.   Pack Light: Choose versatile clothing items that can be mixed and matched to create different outfits.

This packing guide ensures you are well-prepared for your trip to Uzbekistan, making your experience as enjoyable and hassle-free as possible.

Financial Planning

Currency Details

The official currency of Uzbekistan is the Uzbek som (UZS). Here's what you need to know:

1.   **Exchange Rates:** Use online resources to check the latest exchange rates between your home currency and the Uzbek som.

2.   **Cash vs. Cards:** While credit cards are increasingly accepted in major cities, Uzbekistan primarily operates on a cash basis. Make sure you have enough cash for daily expenses, taxis, and smaller shops or restaurants that might not accept cards.

3.   **Currency Exchange:** You can exchange money at the airport upon arrival or at exchange bureaus in major cities. Always use reputable establishments and compare rates before making a transaction. It's also a good idea to exchange some currency before your trip for immediate expenses upon arrival.

Budgeting Suggestions

Uzbekistan caters to a range of budgets. Here are some tips to help you manage your finances:

1. **Accommodation:** Prices vary based on the type of accommodation. Hostels and guesthouses offer budget-friendly options, while mid-range hotels provide comfortable stays. Luxury hotels are available in major cities for those seeking a more lavish experience. Research and book your accommodation in advance, especially during peak seasons.

2. **Transportation:** Public transportation within cities is affordable. Taxis are widely available and reasonably priced, but always agree on the fare beforehand. Consider buying a local SIM card for internet access and using ride-hailing apps if available.

3. **Food:** Uzbek cuisine is flavorful and affordable. Local restaurants and street food stalls offer delicious meals at good prices. Don't forget to include the cost of bottled water in your budget, as staying hydrated is essential, especially in hot weather.

4. **Activities and Attractions:** Entrance fees for museums, historical sites, and other attractions vary. Some places offer discounts for students or seniors. Factor these costs into your itinerary planning.

5. **Shopping:** Uzbekistan has lively bazaars and shops selling souvenirs, handicrafts, and traditional clothing. Set aside a budget for shopping based on your interests.

Haggling is common in bazaars, so be ready to negotiate for the best price.

6. Tipping: Tipping is not a traditional practice in Uzbekistan, but it is becoming more common in tourist areas. A small tip for good service at restaurants or for hotel porters is appreciated.

Saving Strategies

Here are some tips to save money during your Uzbek adventure:

1. Travel During Shoulder Seasons: Consider visiting Uzbekistan in spring (March-May) or autumn (September-November) to avoid peak season crowds and potentially higher prices.

2. Travel with a Companion: Sharing accommodation and transportation costs with a friend or fellow traveler can significantly reduce expenses.

3. Utilize Public Transportation: Public transportation is a cost-effective way to get around cities. Research local routes and buy passes if available for additional savings.

4. Pack Light: Avoid baggage fees by packing light and choosing versatile clothing that can be mixed and matched.

5. Cook Some Meals: If staying in guesthouses with kitchens, consider preparing some meals to save on dining costs. Visit local bazaars for fresh ingredients for an authentic experience.

6. Learn Basic Uzbek Phrases: Learning a few basic Uzbek phrases can help you interact with locals and negotiate better prices at shops and bazaars.

Additional Tips:

1. Research Visa Costs: Include the cost of obtaining a visa for Uzbekistan in your budget.

2. Travel Insurance: Consider getting travel insurance to protect against unexpected medical emergencies or travel disruptions.

3. Set a Daily Budget: Establish a realistic daily budget and track your expenses to avoid overspending.

4. Use Budgeting Apps: Utilize budgeting apps to manage your finances while traveling.

What to Buy and Eat
Food to Try

Uzbekistan, a landlocked country, is known for its rich farmlands that provide a diverse range of food sources, including bread, rice, noodles, and sheep. The country's cuisine offers a variety of flavors and textures, from robust meat dishes to delicate pastries. If you're planning a trip to this intriguing country, experiencing its vibrant and delectable cuisine is a must. Here are ten traditional Uzbek dishes that you should definitely try for an authentic culinary experience.

- ❖ **Plov Plov:** the national dish of Uzbekistan, is a must-try for any visitor. This nutritious rice pilaf is often served at weddings, festivals, and other special occasions, symbolizing generosity and hospitality in Uzbek culture. Plov is prepared by sautéing meat, usually lamb, beef, or chicken, along with onions and carrots in oil or fat. Rice, water or broth, and spices like cumin, coriander, and turmeric are then added. The dish is traditionally cooked in a large cast-iron pot called a 'kazan' over an open flame, which gives it a distinctive smoky flavor. Plov can also include vegetables such as tomatoes, peppers, and garlic and is often served with pickled vegetables, sour cream, or yogurt.

- ❖ **Manti:** is a popular traditional dish in Uzbek cuisine, consisting of dumplings filled with ground meat, usually lamb or beef, mixed with onions and various seasonings.

The dough for the wrappers is made from flour, water, and sometimes eggs. Manti are known for their unique preparation and presentation. They are typically made in small, bite-sized portions and are steamed or boiled. Commonly, manti are arranged on a plate and topped with a garlicky yogurt sauce and a sprinkle of paprika or red pepper flakes. This beloved dish is often enjoyed on special occasions or during family gatherings, with each dumpling handcrafted with care.

- **Lagman:** also known as 'laghman', is another essential dish in Uzbekistan. This noodle dish is made with hand-pulled noodles cooked in a savory broth with meat, such as lamb or beef, vegetables, and a blend of spices like cumin, coriander, and paprika. Lagman can be served as a soup or as a main dish, often accompanied by bread or salad. The rich and complex flavor of the broth makes lagman a comforting and satisfying meal, perfect for warming up on a chilly day.

- **Shashlik:** For meat lovers, shashlik is a must-try in Uzbekistan. This dish consists of skewered and grilled pieces of marinated meat, such as beef, lamb, chicken, or occasionally horse. The meat is cut into bite-sized cubes and marinated with ingredients like garlic, onions, vinegar, and spices. Shashlik is often served with traditional accompaniments like lavash (flatbread), fresh vegetables, and sometimes a yogurt-based sauce called 'suzma'. The simplicity and irresistible flavor of shashlik make it a popular dish at barbecues and outdoor gatherings.

- **Achichuk:** is a refreshing salad made from a simple yet delightful combination of ingredients. It consists of thinly sliced tomatoes, cucumbers, and red onions mixed with fresh herbs. The salad is dressed with a zesty mixture of vinegar, lemon juice, and vegetable oil, which adds a tangy and slightly acidic flavor. Achichuk is often served as a side dish with plov or other Uzbek meals. Its fresh flavors make it an ideal dish to enjoy during the summer.

- **Samsa:** is a savory pastry similar to the Indian samosa, popular as both a snack and street food in Uzbekistan. The pastry is made by filling a thin layer of dough with spiced ground meat, onions, and sometimes potatoes or pumpkin. The dough is then molded into a triangular shape and baked in a tandoor, a special clay oven, until golden brown and crispy. Samsa is a staple in Uzbek cuisine and is often served hot with tea or a cold beverage, making it a perfect choice for breakfast or a quick snack.

- **Obi Non:** is a round flatbread that is a staple in Uzbekistan. This bread is characterized by its unique surface, decorated with intricate designs made by pressing the dough with a special tool called a 'chekich'. Obi Non is traditionally baked in a tandoor oven or on a flat griddle, resulting in a slightly chewy surface and a crispy bottom. Each town and region in Uzbekistan has its own way of making Obi Non. This versatile bread can be eaten with almost everything, from scooping up stews and dips to accompanying other dishes.

- **Chuchvara:** often called Uzbek dumplings, are small, bite-sized dumplings filled with minced meat (like beef or lamb), chopped onions, and aromatic spices. These dumplings are boiled in water until tender and cooked through. Chuchvara is typically served in soup as a main dish or an appetizer, but it can also be fried. This meal is especially popular in cold weather and is often enjoyed with friends and family.

- **Shurpa:** is a hearty soup made by simmering meat, such as lamb or beef, with onions, carrots, potatoes, and various spices. The spices and slow simmering process give shurpa a distinct and aromatic flavor. The meat is simmered until tender, allowing the broth to be infused with its flavor, and then vegetables are added to enhance the taste and texture. Shurpa is often served with fresh bread, making it a fulfilling and comforting dish.

- **Shivit Oshi:** is one of the most vibrant dishes in Uzbekistan, representing the country's rich culinary heritage. This dish consists of green noodles that are cooked until tender and served with various vegetables, topped with meat, typically lamb or beef. The meat is cooked until tender and combined with other ingredients to create a rich and flavorful sauce. Shivit Oshi is also garnished with an assortment of vegetables, including bell peppers, carrots, and onions, creating a visually striking and delicious meal.

Things to Buy When Touring Uzbekistan

Uzbekistan, a country steeped in history and culture, offers a wide array of unique and authentic items that make perfect souvenirs or gifts. From detailed textiles and ceramics to traditional jewelry and spices, the markets and shops in Uzbekistan are brimming with treasures that reflect the country's diverse heritage. Here's a guide on what to buy when visiting Uzbekistan.

- ❖ **Suzani Embroideries:** Suzani, a type of embroidered textile from Uzbekistan, is known for its complex patterns and vibrant colors. Traditionally handmade, suzanis feature floral and geometric designs and are often used as wall hangings, bedspreads, or tablecloths. When buying a suzani, look for pieces that display detailed craftsmanship and vivid colors. High-quality suzanis can be found in bazaars and specialized shops in cities like Samarkand, Bukhara, and Tashkent.

- ❖ **Ceramics and Pottery:** Uzbekistan is famous for its beautifully crafted ceramics, particularly from the cities of Rishtan and Gijduvan. These ceramics are characterized by their bright blue and green glazes and intricate patterns. Popular items include plates, bowls, vases, and tiles. Each piece is typically hand-painted, making every item unique. When buying ceramics, consider visiting workshops where you can see artisans at work and buy directly from them.

- ❖ **Handwoven Carpets and Rugs:** Uzbekistan's carpets and rugs are known for their quality and intricate designs. Bukhara and Samarkand are famous for their handwoven carpets, which often feature traditional patterns and vibrant colors. When buying a carpet, consider its origin, the materials used (wool or silk), and the knot density, which indicates the quality and durability. Authentic Uzbek carpets can be a bit pricey, but they are worth the investment for their beauty and craftsmanship.

- ❖ **Traditional Jewelry:** Uzbek jewelry reflects the country's rich cultural heritage. Silver and gold jewelry adorned with semi-precious stones like turquoise, lapis lazuli, and carnelian are popular. Traditional designs often include intricate filigree work and are inspired by the region's historical influences. You can find beautiful pieces in local markets, and it's advisable to buy from reputable sellers to ensure authenticity.

- ❖ **Ikats and Silk Products:** Ikat, known locally as "abrband," is a type of fabric that features a distinctive tie-dye pattern. The Fergana Valley, particularly the city of Margilan, is renowned for its ikat production. Silk and cotton ikat fabrics are used to make scarves, robes, and clothing. These vibrant textiles make excellent gifts and can be found in markets and boutique shops throughout Uzbekistan.

- ❖ **Miniature Paintings:** Inspired by the Persian miniature tradition, Uzbek miniature paintings are detailed artworks depicting historical scenes, landscapes, and traditional life. These paintings are often done on paper or camel bone and make for beautiful decorative pieces. The city of Bukhara is particularly known for its miniature paintings, and you can find them in art galleries and souvenir shops.

- ❖ **Traditional Musical Instruments For music enthusiasts:** traditional Uzbek musical instruments make for a unique and meaningful souvenir. Instruments like the doira (a type of frame drum), dutar (a two-stringed lute), and rubab (a plucked string instrument) are not only beautiful but also hold cultural significance. These can be found in markets and music shops, especially in larger cities like Tashkent and Samarkand.

- ❖ **Spices and Teas:** Uzbekistan's markets are filled with an array of aromatic spices and teas. Popular spices include saffron, cumin, coriander, and dried chilies. You can also find special blends used in traditional dishes like plov. Additionally, Uzbekistan has a rich tea culture, and you can purchase green tea and herbal blends that are commonly enjoyed throughout the country. Spices and teas make for practical and fragrant souvenirs.

- **Leather Goods:** Uzbekistan produces high-quality leather goods, including bags, belts, and footwear. The leather is often hand-stitched and features traditional designs. Bukhara is particularly known for its leather products, and you can find a variety of items in local shops and markets.

- **Papier-mâché Items:** Papier-mâché is a traditional craft in Uzbekistan, used to create decorative items like masks, boxes, and figurines. These items are often painted with intricate designs and make for charming and lightweight souvenirs. You can find papier-mâché crafts in many markets and artisan shops, especially in the cultural hubs of Samarkand and Bukhara.

Tips for Shopping in Uzbekistan

Bargaining: Haggling is a common practice in Uzbek markets, so don't hesitate to negotiate the price. However, do so respectfully and with a smile.

Authenticity: To ensure you're buying authentic items, consider purchasing from reputable shops or directly from artisans.

Transport: Keep in mind the size and weight of items, especially if you're traveling by air. Many shops offer shipping services if you purchase larger items like carpets or ceramics.

Cash: While credit cards are becoming more widely accepted, it's best to carry cash, especially in local markets and smaller shops.

CHAPTER FOUR

Uzbekistan Cities

Tashkent

Tashkent, the capital of Uzbekistan, may not initially enchant you like its Silk Road siblings - Khiva, Bukhara, and Samarkand. However, its unique and peculiar allure is sure to win you over!

One might question why Tashkent lacks the historical richness of Khiva, Samarkand, and Bukhara, which are brimming with historical gems. The answer is simple: Tashkent was designated as the capital city of the Autonomous Soviet Socialist Republic of Turkestan by the Soviets in 1918, a relatively late development.

Moreover, in April 1966, a devastating earthquake hit the city, wiping out entire neighborhoods. This led to a significant rebuilding effort during the 1960s and 1970s, which bestowed upon the Uzbek capital its unmistakable Soviet flavor.

Present-day Tashkent is a city that merits recognition. Its hospitable inhabitants, delectable eateries, fascinating landmarks, and remarkable historical structures make it a worthwhile destination for a day or two.

Origin story

Tashkent, the current capital of Uzbekistan, has a history that extends over two millennia. Its earliest mentions are found in Chinese records, where it was referred to as Shi, Chzhemi, or Yueni. Another ancient name, Shash-Tepa (or Chach-Tepa), can be traced back to the 2nd to 1st centuries BC. During the early Middle Ages, it was known as Binkent. From the 11th century onwards, it has been known as Tashkent, which means "stone city" in Uzbek, derived from "tosch" (stone) and "kent" (city).

The first urban settlement appeared in the 4th and 5th centuries. Archaeological discoveries from this era, such as bronze mirrors and coins from various early civilizations, were found in burial mounds. In the 6th century, the city, then known as Chacha, was taken over by the Turkic Kaganate, which later fragmented into smaller territories in the 7th century.

The next rulers of Tashkent were the Arabs, who conquered Central Asia. They renamed the city Binkent and began the imposition of Islam, often eradicating local cultural practices. After two centuries of Arab rule, Tashkent became part of the Samanid state in the 9th century. From the 10th to the 13th centuries, it was governed by the Kara-Khanids and the Kara-Khitans (Hala Qidans).

In the early 13th century, Tashkent fell to Genghis Khan, leading to a period of decline. However, with the arrival of new settlers, Tashkent began to grow again. In the 14th century, it was conquered by Amir Temur (Tamerlane) and became a significant fortress of the Temurid state.

In the latter half of the 16th century, Tashkent became part of the Bukhara Khanate, and in 1809 it was annexed by the Khanate of Kokand. During this period, the city expanded and became a major trade center with Russia.

In 1865, Tashkent was taken by Russian troops, along with many other areas of Central Asia. Russian settlers began building the New Town, which was separated from the Old Town by the Anchor canal. The Old Town was mainly inhabited by artisans and merchants, while the New City, built among gardens and fields, became the industrial center. At the same time, Tashkent became the main city of the Turkestan general-governorship.

After the October Revolution in Russia in 1917, Tashkent was declared the capital of the Turkestan Autonomous Soviet Socialist Republic. In 1924, with the creation of the Uzbek SSR, the capital moved to Samarkand, but in 1930, it was returned to Tashkent.

During World War II, Tashkent became a significant evacuation center. The city's defense industries rapidly grew, and many theaters, movie studios, and leading figures of Russian science and culture were relocated there. This influx significantly influenced the city's development. During the war, Tashkent provided shelter and sustenance to hundreds of thousands of people, earning the nickname "Tashkent – the City of Bread."

In 1966, a major earthquake devastated much of the city. The rest of the USSR came to Tashkent's aid, and within a few years, the city was rebuilt.

After gaining independence in 1991, Tashkent remained the capital of the Republic of Uzbekistan. In 1983, Tashkent celebrated its 2,000th anniversary, and in 2009, after new archaeological research, it celebrated its 2,200th anniversary.

Today, Tashkent is a bustling city with over 2 million residents and is one of the largest cities in Central Asia. It is a city of contrasts, where you can see a blend of East and West: traditional bazaars and modern supermarkets, old neighborhoods (mahallas) and high-rise buildings, and many other interesting combinations.

Getting to Tashkent

From France:

Travelers from France can reach Tashkent via direct or indirect flights from Paris Charles de Gaulle airport. Uzbekistan Airways offers direct flights, while Air Astana provides flights with a layover in Astana, Kazakhstan. Direct flights typically take around 7 hours, whereas flights with layovers take approximately 11 hours. Using Skyscanner to book your flights is advisable, as it allows you to compare prices and flight options by date and airline to find the best deal.

From Other Cities in Uzbekistan:

Tashkent is well-connected to other cities in Uzbekistan, with various transportation options available:

• **Air Travel:** This is a convenient option, especially if you're traveling from Urgench (near Khiva) or Bukhara. Domestic flights are reasonably priced, with tickets ranging from €30-€50 from Bukhara and €50-€75 from Urgench.

• **Train Travel:** Fast trains run from Bukhara, Samarkand, and even the Ferghana Valley to Tashkent. This is a quick and relatively affordable way to travel.

• **Private or Shared Taxis:** These are available from Samarkand and the Ferghana Valley, providing a flexible travel option.

From Kyrgyzstan, Kazakhstan, or Tajikistan:

If you're traveling from nearby countries like Kyrgyzstan, Kazakhstan, or Tajikistan, reaching Tashkent is straightforward. Regular flights connect the Uzbek capital to Bishkek, Almaty, and Dushanbe, making it easy to get to Tashkent from these neighboring cities.

Getting around Uzbek

Taxis in Tashkent

Hailing a taxi is the easiest way to navigate Tashkent, and it's surprisingly economical. For city trips, you can anticipate paying between 10,000 and 20,000 soums (roughly 1 to 2 euros). There are two kinds of taxis: official taxis, which are a bit pricier, and unofficial taxis. To hail a taxi, simply stand by the side of the road and raise your hand. In Tashkent, it's common to flag down any car, not just those that resemble traditional taxis. Local drivers are used to stopping to pick up passengers for a nominal fee. If your destination is not on their route, they will kindly decline the ride.

It's not uncommon for drivers to ask you to propose a fare. If they don't, feel free to negotiate a fair price. Bargaining is a common practice and is generally accepted.

Tashkent Metro

While a metro station may not always be close to your starting point, the Tashkent Metro can be a handy and efficient means of transport, particularly for getting to popular spots like Amir Timur Square and Chorsu Market. Metro tickets are extremely affordable, costing only 1,200 soums, which is just a few cents. However, be aware that photography inside the metro is not allowed, as I learned from experience.

Exploring Tashkent by Bus

For a more organized way to explore the city, you can take a tourist bus that offers tours starting from Amir Timur Square. For more details and to catch the bus, head to the square in front of the Uzbekistan Hotel. This bus tour is an excellent way to get a glimpse of Tashkent's main attractions and landmarks.

Lodging Options in Tashkent

Are you searching for a place to stay in Tashkent? Here are some suggestions for various budgets, ensuring a pleasant stay during your tour of Uzbekistan.

Budget Lodging

Topchan Hostel:

- **Location:** Positioned near Tashkent's center, offering easy access to numerous local attractions.
- **Features:** The hostel provides rooms in dormitory style and private rooms, all with shared bathrooms. Amenities include complimentary Wi-Fi, a shared kitchen, a lounge area with a TV, and a garden for relaxation.
- **Offers:** Guests can enjoy a free breakfast, and the hostel organizes various social activities for travelers to interact.
- **Price Range:** Rates begin from around $10-15 per night for a bed in a dormitory, making it an excellent choice for budget-conscious travelers.

Art Hostel:

- **Location:** Situated in a peaceful neighborhood, Art Hostel is a short distance from Tashkent's city center and near public transport.
- **Features:** The hostel offers both dormitory beds and private rooms. It has an outdoor pool, a shared kitchen, and a cozy common area with artistic decor.
- **Offers:** Free breakfast, Wi-Fi, and bicycle rentals. The hostel also hosts art events and workshops.
- **Price Range:** Dormitory beds start at around $12 per night, with private rooms available for approximately $25-30 per night.

Amir Khan Hostel:

- **Location:** Conveniently located near Chorsu Bazaar, one of Tashkent's most famous markets.
- **Features:** The hostel offers a mix of dormitory and private rooms, a shared kitchen, and a common lounge area. The atmosphere is friendly and welcoming.
- **Offers:** Free breakfast, Wi-Fi, and parking. The staff can also help arrange tours and transport.
- **Price Range:** Prices start from $10 per night for a dorm bed, with private rooms costing around $20-25 per night.

Mid-Range Lodging

Meros Boutique Hotel:

- **Location:** Centrally located, offering easy access to Tashkent's main attractions and business areas.
- **Features:** The hotel features stylishly decorated rooms with modern amenities including air conditioning, flat-screen TVs, and private bathrooms. There's also an on-site restaurant serving local and international cuisine.
- **Offers:** Guests can enjoy free Wi-Fi, breakfast, and airport shuttle services. The hotel also has a business center and meeting rooms.
- **Price Range:** Room rates start at approximately $60-80 per night, providing great value for money with its amenities and location.

ART Hotel:

- **Location:** In the heart of Tashkent, close to popular landmarks such as Independence Square and Amir Timur Museum.
- **Features:** The hotel offers well-furnished rooms with contemporary decor, air conditioning, and private bathrooms. There is an on-site cafe, a fitness center, and a garden.
- **Offers:** Complimentary breakfast and Wi-Fi, along with free parking. The hotel staff are helpful and can assist with travel arrangements.
- **Price Range:** Prices range from $50-70 per night, making it a solid choice for mid-range travelers.

Tourist Inn Hotel:

- ❖ **Location:** Situated near Tashkent International Airport, Tourist Inn Hotel is perfect for travelers looking for convenience and comfort.
- ❖ **Features:** The hotel features clean, comfortable rooms equipped with all necessary amenities. There's also a restaurant, a bar, and a 24-hour front desk.
- ❖ **Offers:** Free Wi-Fi, breakfast, and airport transfer services. The hotel also offers laundry and concierge services.
- ❖ **Price Range:** Room rates start at around $55-75 per night.

Luxury Lodging

Wyndham Tashkent:

- ❖ **Location:** Located in the business district, close to key attractions like the Amir Timur Museum and the State Museum of History of Uzbekistan.
- ❖ **Features:** This luxurious hotel offers spacious rooms and suites with elegant decor, flat-screen TVs, minibars, and marble bathrooms. The hotel boasts multiple dining options, a fitness center, a spa, and an indoor pool.
- ❖ **Offers:** Free Wi-Fi, breakfast buffet, and extensive business facilities. The hotel also provides airport shuttle services and concierge assistance.

- **Price Range:** Rates start at around $150-200 per night, reflecting the high level of service and amenities.

Aster Hotel:

- **Location:** Located in a prime area of Tashkent, within easy reach of major tourist spots and shopping centers.
- **Features:** The hotel features luxurious rooms and suites with modern furnishings, including air conditioning, satellite TV, and private bathrooms with premium toiletries. There is an on-site gourmet restaurant, a rooftop bar, and a wellness center with a gym and sauna.
- **Offers:** Complimentary breakfast, Wi-Fi, and valet parking. The hotel also offers personalized concierge services and tour arrangements.
- **Price Range:** Prices typically range from $130-180 per night, providing a luxurious experience with exceptional service.

Each of these lodging options in Tashkent offers unique features and amenities catering to different budgets, ensuring a comfortable and enjoyable stay in the city.

Dining Options in Tashkent

Tashkent offers a lively food scene that combines traditional Uzbek meals with global cuisine. Here are five dining establishments that provide a range of culinary experiences, from economical choices to luxurious venues, catering to diverse tastes and budgets.

Caravan Restaurant

- ❖ **Location:** 22 Abdulla Kadiry Street, Tashkent
- ❖ **Atmosphere:** Caravan Restaurant exudes a warm and traditional ambiance, decorated with local crafts and tapestries that create a genuine Uzbek environment. The restaurant offers both indoor seating and a charming outdoor terrace for open-air dining.
- ❖ **Food:** The menu features classic Uzbek meals such as plov, shashlik, and manti, along with a variety of international dishes. Vegetarian options are also available.
- ❖ **Unique Features:** Live music performances add to the dining experience, creating a vibrant and entertaining atmosphere. The restaurant also offers cooking classes for those interested in learning how to make Uzbek meals.
- ❖ **Price Range:** Prices are moderate, with main dishes typically costing between $10 and $20.

Afsona Restaurant

- ❖ **Location:** 1 Istiklol Street, Tashkent

- **Atmosphere:** Afsona Restaurant has a modern design with elements of traditional Uzbek decor. The interior is elegant and sophisticated, making it an excellent choice for a more upscale dining experience.
- **Food:** The menu presents a contemporary interpretation of traditional Uzbek cuisine, with dishes like quail with pomegranate sauce and lamb cooked in a tandoor oven. There is also a good selection of local wines.
- **Unique Features:** The restaurant provides a comprehensive dining experience with attentive service and a well-curated menu. Private dining rooms are available for special occasions.
- **Price Range:** Afsona is on the higher end, with main courses ranging from $15 to $30.

Plov-Samsa Centre

- **Location:** 35 Alisher Navoi Street, Tashkent
- **Atmosphere:** This casual eatery is a local favorite for its simple and unassuming setting. The focus here is on delivering the best versions of traditional dishes.
- **Food:** As the name suggests, the specialty here is plov, the national dish of Uzbekistan, and samsa, a type of pastry filled with meat or vegetables. The menu is simple, focusing on a few staple dishes done exceptionally well.
- **Unique Features:** Quick service and a friendly atmosphere make it ideal for a casual meal. It's a

great place to experience authentic Uzbek food at an affordable price.
- ❖ **Price Range:** Very budget-friendly, with meals typically costing between $5 and $10.

Jumanji Restaurant

- ❖ **Location:** 7 Taras Shevchenko Street, Tashkent
- ❖ **Atmosphere:** Jumanji Restaurant is known for its vibrant and eclectic decor, featuring a mix of jungle themes and modern design elements. The atmosphere is lively and fun, perfect for families and groups.
- ❖ **Food:** The menu offers a wide variety of dishes, including European, Asian, and Uzbek cuisine. Popular items include sushi, pizza, and traditional kebabs.
- ❖ **Unique Features:** The restaurant frequently hosts themed nights and entertainment events, making it a dynamic spot for a night out. There's also a children's play area, making it family-friendly.
- ❖ **Price Range:** Mid-range, with main dishes priced between $10 and $25.

Navvat Lounge & Restaurant

- ❖ **Location:** 10 Amir Timur Street, Tashkent
- ❖ **Atmosphere:** Navvat Lounge & Restaurant offers a stylish and modern dining environment with a chic interior. The rooftop seating area provides a stunning view of the city, especially beautiful in the evening.

- **Food:** The menu features a fusion of Mediterranean and Uzbek dishes, with options like grilled meats, seafood, and various mezes. The dessert selection includes traditional sweets and contemporary creations.
- **Unique Features:** The restaurant has a well-stocked bar with an extensive selection of cocktails and wines. Live DJ performances and themed nights add to the vibrant nightlife experience.
- **Price Range:** Higher-end, with main courses ranging from $20 to $35.

These dining establishments in Tashkent offer a range of culinary experiences, from traditional Uzbek cuisine to international fare, catering to different budgets and preferences.

Sights in Tashkent

Amir Timur Square and Its Environs

Amir Timur Square is a spacious plaza where several of Tashkent's main thoroughfares converge. While the square itself may not be particularly eye-catching, the area around it offers plenty to discover. Here, you'll find some of the city's most significant landmarks, such as the Uzbekistan Art Gallery and the Monument of the Grieving Mother.

The square is encircled by lush greenery, making it a delightful spot for a stroll and for observing people. It's a common sight to see locals engaged in a game of chess or simply relaxing in the area. The surrounding environment is filled with trees and greenery, offering a tranquil atmosphere amidst the urban landscape.

The Square's Architecture Amir Timur Square exudes a distinct Soviet-era feel, characterized by its majestic buildings with commanding silhouettes. One of the most notable structures is the vast Hotel Uzbekistan. At the center of the square stands a large equestrian statue of Tamerlane, also known as Amir Timur, who is a revered national hero in Uzbekistan.

In the past, the square was graced with ancient plane trees. However, these were felled in 2010 by the order of former Uzbek President Islam Karimov. The exact reasons for this decision remain unclear, but it is speculated that he wanted to accentuate the Dom Forum, a massive hall constructed in 2009 for high-profile events and occasional concerts.

The Amir Timur Museum Situated near the square

The Amir Timur Museum is entirely dedicated to Tamerlane and his descendants. The museum seeks to draw parallels between this historical figure and the current government of Uzbekistan. While the presentation may lack objectivity, the museum provides a comprehensive overview of the turbulent history of this formidable conqueror.

If Tashkent is your first stop in Uzbekistan, a visit to the Amir Timur Museum can be a great introduction to the country's rich history. Tamerlane's influence is evident throughout Uzbekistan, and understanding his legacy can enhance your appreciation of the country's culture and historical sites.

The Photography House For photography enthusiasts

The Photography House is a must-visit. This museum offers a unique perspective on Uzbekistan through the works of contemporary Uzbek photographers. It provides an excellent opportunity to see the country through the eyes of local artists, showcasing everyday life and the beauty of the region from a fresh, modern viewpoint. Exploring these attractions around Amir Timur Square will give you a deeper insight into Tashkent's cultural and historical landscape, making your visit to the Uzbek capital a more enriching experience.

The Uzbekistan Art Gallery

The Uzbekistan Art Gallery, which opened its doors in 2004, is a treasure trove of artistic expression. It showcases a wide range of works created by Uzbek artists, spanning from the 20th century up to the present day. This gallery offers a comprehensive look at the evolution of Uzbek art over the years. Inside the gallery, you'll find an extensive collection that includes paintings, sculptures, and various forms of contemporary art. The works reflect the diverse cultural heritage and artistic traditions of Uzbekistan. The pieces on display are not only visually stunning but also provide insight into the social and historical context in which they were created.

The gallery is conveniently located, making it easily accessible for both locals and tourists. As you wander through the exhibits, you'll encounter a rich array of styles and mediums. From traditional motifs and techniques to modern and abstract interpretations, the gallery captures the dynamic and evolving nature of Uzbek art. Visiting the Uzbekistan Art Gallery is an enriching experience that allows you to appreciate the creativity and talent of Uzbek artists. It serves as a platform for both established and emerging artists to present their work, fostering a vibrant artistic community. Whether you're an art enthusiast or a casual visitor, the gallery offers something for everyone, providing a deeper understanding of the artistic landscape of Uzbekistan.

Mustaqillik Maidoni

The Independence Square Mustaqillik Maidoni, or Independence Square, is a must-see destination in Tashkent. Spanning nearly 12 hectares, this vast, tree-lined square was known as "Lenin Square" until the Soviet Union's dissolution. In 1991, following Uzbekistan's independence, it was renamed "Independence Square," and the colossal statue of Lenin that once dominated its center was replaced by the equally grand "Independence Monument."

The square is a blend of greenery and striking architectural features. Its paved areas are adorned with giant fountains that create a mesmerizing sight, especially when illuminated at night. Overlooking these fountains is a grand portico topped with statues of pelicans, which are symbols of good fortune in Uzbek culture.

Monument of the Grieving Mother

The Mustaqillik Maidoni is home to the touching Monument of the Grieving Mother, a tribute to the 400,000 Uzbek soldiers who lost their lives in World War II. Erected in 1999, the monument features a statue of a grieving woman, guarded by an eternal flame. The names of the fallen soldiers are carefully etched on large metal plaques, resembling giant books, housed within two colonnaded galleries on either side of the statue. This memorial serves as a solemn reminder of the sacrifices made during the war.

The Romanov Palace

The Romanov Palace, a stunning building from the Tsarist era, is a sight to behold in Tashkent. Although it's not open to the public, its historical charm can be admired from the gated entrance. The palace is set within a lush garden, adding to its allure. Its inaccessibility lends an air of mystery and intrigue, making it a point of interest for those keen on exploring Uzbekistan's rich past.

Navoi Park

Navoi Park, located to the west of Tashkent, offers a unique view of the city's diverse landscape. The park is a blend of well-kept areas and sections that appear to be overlooked. Wide paved roads, mostly devoid of vehicles, crisscross the park, adding to its mystique.

Within the park, you'll find several impressive and somewhat lavish buildings. Among these are the striking Istiqlol Palace, previously known as the Palace of Friendship of Peoples, and the Wedding Palace, a symbol of love and celebration. The Lower Chamber of Parliament, which primarily serves to register presidential decrees, adds a hint of political history to the park's varied mix.

In contrast to these grand structures, the monument to Alisher Navoi offers a tranquil retreat. Nestled among trees and flowers, this tribute to the famous poet and philosopher provides a peaceful sanctuary within the park, a stark contrast to the imposing buildings that surround it.

While Navoi Park may not seem extraordinary at first glance, a leisurely walk through its grounds offers a fascinating and unusual view of the Uzbek capital. It's a worthwhile stop for those keen on exploring the city's hidden gems and experiencing its diverse character.

Chorsu Bazaar

Located in the northwest part of Tashkent, Chorsu Bazaar is a vibrant market under a large green dome, offering a taste of Uzbek culture. The market is filled with a variety of spices, meats, breads, pastries, cheeses, fruits, and vegetables, all beautifully arranged in bustling stalls along narrow lanes. The streets around the bazaar are equally vibrant, with many vendors selling a range of goods.

Chorsu Bazaar is also a great place for souvenir shopping. The variety of products is vast, and the atmosphere is captivating. I found it hard to resist buying assortments of spices and sweets to take home.

A short distance from Chorsu Bazaar, you'll find the Juma Mosque and Kulkedash Madrasa, both located on a hill. The Juma Mosque, originally built in 819, has undergone several reconstructions, with the most recent significant restoration taking place in the 1990s, after the Soviet era when the mosque had been used as office space.

Next to the mosque, the Kulkedash Madrasa, established in 1570, stands as a testament to the city's historical depth. In the 19th century, it served as a fortress for the Khans of Kokand. Later, it was restored to its original function as a Quranic school and continues to serve as an educational institution today.

Northeast of Chorsu Bazaar is Khast Imam Square, the spiritual center of Uzbekistan. This beautifully restored square offers visitors a serene atmosphere and a deeper understanding of the country's spiritual heritage.

Whether you're admiring the historic Juma Mosque, exploring the educational legacy of the Kulkedash Madrasa, or soaking in the spiritual ambiance of Khast Imam Square, the area around Chorsu Bazaar offers a rich and immersive experience of Tashkent's culture and history.

Hazrati Imam Friday Mosque

The Hazrati Imam Friday Mosque, built in 2007 under the directive of former President Islam Karimov, mirrors the architectural style of 16th-century mosques. The mosque, topped with a striking blue dome and flanked by two tall minarets, showcases intricate sculptures that exemplify the finest traditions of Uzbek craftsmanship.

Tamerlane

Built in the 16th century by a descendant of Ulugbek, who was himself a descendant of the legendary Tamerlane, the Barak Khan Madrasa is one of the most exquisite landmarks in the capital. In a transformation seen in many historical madrasas in Uzbekistan, the students' quarters have been converted into shops.

Museum-Library Moyie Mubarek

Located opposite the madrasa, the Museum-Library Moyie Mubarek is famous for housing the Osman Quran, believed to be the oldest Quran in existence. Legend has it that this sacred text was brought to Tamerlane during one of his conquests and later seized by the Soviets, only to be returned by Lenin as an act of goodwill. The museum-library also features a collection of rare books, including some remarkably small copies of the Quran, making it quite unique.

Mausoleum of Abou Bakr Kaffal Chachi

A short walk through a lush park leads to the Mausoleum of Abou Bakr Kaffal Chachi, which contains the tomb of the esteemed poet and Islamic scholar, revered as the patron saint of Tashkent. Built in 1541, this mausoleum is a significant pilgrimage site for Muslims.

Cheikhantaur Ensemble

North of Navoi Boulevard lies the Cheikhantaur Ensemble, a collection of three ancient mausoleums within the Islamic University of Tashkent campus. Unfortunately, only two of these mausoleums are accessible to the public, while the third, the Yunus Khan Mausoleum, can only be viewed from a distance. The accessible mausoleums are set in a small, tree-lined garden: the Kaldirgochbiy Mausoleum, notable for its unique pyramidal roof, and the Sheikh Hovendi Takhur Mausoleum, distinguished by its dome. Nearby, there is also a beautiful mosque.

Ugam-Chatkal

Located about 100 kilometers from Tashkent, Ugam-Chatkal National Park is a great place to get some fresh air and enjoy outdoor activities. The park is about a 1 hour 15-45 minute drive from the city. You can spend a few days here or just take a day trip, which costs around $80 for a car. To book your trip, you can ask your hotel in Tashkent, as most hotels can make the reservation for you. Alternatively, local agencies can help, especially if you're interested in hiking or other outdoor activities.

The park is a haven for sports lovers, offering skiing in the winter, trekking, and rafting. For organizing these activities, consider using local agencies like Asia Adventures or Asian Special Tourism.

Lake Charvak

Lake Charvak is situated a short distance from Bel'dersay. This man-made lake, complete with a remarkable dam, is a sight to behold. It's worth noting that the current President of Uzbekistan, Shavkat Mirziyoyev, has a retreat in the vicinity of this lake. The landscape is undeniably beautiful, but it's advisable not to spend too much time here. The area is filled with water sports facilities that are often crowded and not in the best condition, which can detract from the overall enjoyment of the place.

CHAPTER FIVE

The Fergana Valley of Uzbekistan

Namangan

Namangan city is known for its rich cultural heritage and historical significance. As one of the largest cities in the valley with a population of over 500,000, Namangan is a bustling hub with a diverse economy that includes textiles, food processing, and manufacturing industries. The city is also a center for education and culture, housing several universities and cultural institutions.

Namangan offers a range of attractions, from historical sites to beautiful gardens.

Some of the Main Highlights Include

Babur Park: Named after the renowned Mughal emperor Babur, who was born in the Fergana Valley, this park is a popular spot for locals and tourists alike. It's known for its lush greenery, walking paths, and peaceful atmosphere. The park is a perfect place for families to spend an afternoon, with plenty of space for children to play and adults to relax. It also hosts cultural events and festivals, providing a window into local traditions and customs.

Mulla Kyrgyz Madrasa: This 19th-century educational institution is a significant landmark in Namangan. It showcases traditional Islamic architecture with its beautiful facade decorated with intricate tile work and calligraphy.

Although it no longer operates as a religious school, it remains an important cultural and historical site. Visitors can explore the courtyard and admire the craftsmanship of its construction.

Namangan Central Bazaar: This vibrant market is a must-visit for those looking to experience local culture and buy traditional goods. The market offers a wide variety of products, from fresh produce and spices to handmade crafts and textiles. The lively atmosphere and friendly vendors make it a great place to shop and explore. Visitors can also try local delicacies and street food, offering a unique culinary experience.

Kasansay Canyon: Located just outside Namangan, this natural area features dramatic rock formations and a flowing river. It's a great spot for hiking, picnicking, and enjoying scenic views. The canyon is home to various wildlife, making it an ideal place for bird watching and photography.

Namangan Regional Studies Museum: This museum offers a deeper understanding of Namangan's history and culture. It houses a diverse collection of artifacts, including ancient manuscripts, traditional clothing, and archaeological finds. The museum hosts temporary exhibitions and educational programs, making it an engaging destination for visitors of all ages.

Atavulla Eshan Madrasa: This late 19th-century madrasa is another significant historic site in Namangan. It served as an important center of Islamic learning and its architecture reflects the intricate design elements of the period. Today, it stands as a testament to the city's educational and religious history.

Namangan Floral Park: Known for its beautiful gardens and floral displays, Namangan is a city that celebrates nature. Namangan Floral Park, with its wide variety of flowers and plants, is a popular spot among locals and tourists, especially during the spring and summer months when the flowers are in full bloom.

Abul Kasim Madrasa: This 18th-century madrasa is another historic educational institution worth visiting. Although it no longer serves its original purpose, it remains an important cultural landmark. The madrasa is often used for cultural events and exhibitions, allowing visitors to appreciate its historical and architectural significance.

Andijan

Andijan, located in the eastern part of Uzbekistan, is a city steeped in history and rich in cultural heritage. As one of the oldest cities in the Fergana Valley, Andijan has long been a hub for trade, culture, and education. With a population exceeding 400,000, it's also one of the region's largest cities. Andijan is notably the birthplace of Babur, the founder of the Mughal Empire in India, which adds to its historical significance. The city is home to numerous historical sites and attractions that draw visitors from all over the world.

Historical Landmarks in Andijan

Andijan boasts several historical landmarks that reflect its rich history and cultural heritage. Some of the main historical sites that visitors should explore include:

Jami Madrasah: This large Islamic school, established in the 19th century, is a significant landmark in Andijan. The madrasah showcases traditional Islamic architecture with its stunning facade decorated with intricate tile work and calligraphy. Although it no longer operates as an educational institution, the Jami Madrasah remains an important cultural and historical site. Visitors can explore the courtyard and admire the architectural details of this site.

Andijan Regional Studies Museum: To gain a deeper understanding of Andijan's history and culture, a visit to the Andijan Regional Studies Museum is recommended. The museum houses a diverse collection of artifacts, including archaeological finds, traditional clothing, and ancient manuscripts. The museum offers educational programs and temporary exhibitions, making it an informative and engaging destination for visitors of all ages.

Khanabad Palace: This palace, once the residence of the local khans or rulers, is another notable historical site in Andijan. The palace showcases the architectural styles of the period and features beautiful gardens, intricate woodwork, and stunning tile decorations. Visitors can tour the palace grounds and learn about the history of the local rulers.

Key Highlights of Andijan In addition to its historical sites, Andijan offers several key highlights that showcase the city's vibrant culture and natural beauty. Some of the main attractions include:

Andijan Bazaar: This vibrant marketplace is a must-visit for those looking to experience local culture and buy traditional goods. The bazaar offers a wide variety of products, from fresh produce and spices to handmade crafts and textiles. The lively atmosphere and the colorful array of products make it a must-visit destination in Andijan.

Andijan State University: This leading educational institution in the region is known for its beautiful architecture and well-maintained gardens. Visitors can walk around the campus, admire the historic buildings, and get a sense of the academic atmosphere. The university also hosts various cultural and academic events, making it an important center of learning and culture in Andijan.

Yuldosh Akhunbabaev Memorial Complex: This complex is dedicated to the prominent Uzbek statesman Yuldosh Akhunbabaev. The complex includes a museum, a library, and a memorial statue. The museum houses a collection of artifacts related to Akhunbabaev's life and work, providing insight into his contributions to the development of the region. The memorial complex is an important cultural site and a place of reflection for visitors.

Fergana City

Situated in the eastern part of Uzbekistan, Fergana is a city that is well-known for its deep cultural roots, historical significance, and lively community life. Serving as the administrative center of the Fergana Region, it acts as a crucial hub in the fertile Fergana Valley, one of the most densely populated and agriculturally prosperous areas in Central Asia. With a population of around 250,000, Fergana offers a unique blend of traditional and modern experiences to both its residents and visitors. The city is characterized by its beautiful tree-lined streets, well-maintained parks, and a welcoming atmosphere that mirrors the friendliness of its people.

City Characteristics of Fergana

The city's design and architecture reflect its historical evolution and diverse cultural influences. Fergana is planned with wide boulevards, numerous public squares, and plenty of green spaces, creating a pleasant environment for exploration.

- ❖ **Tree-Lined Streets and Boulevards:** One of the distinguishing features of Fergana is its tree-lined streets and wide boulevards. These green pathways provide shade and visual appeal, making the city conducive for walking and exploration. The streets are alive with activity, with vendors selling fresh produce and handmade crafts, and residents going about their daily lives. The greenery and open spaces contribute to the city's relaxed and inviting atmosphere.

- **Public Parks and Gardens:** Fergana is home to several well-kept parks and gardens, offering spaces for residents and visitors to enjoy nature. These green spaces are perfect for leisurely walks, picnics, and family outings. The parks, with their landscaped gardens, fountains, and playgrounds, are popular spots for families. The focus on public green spaces underscores the city's commitment to ensuring a high quality of life.

- **Cultural and Educational Institutions:** Fergana houses numerous cultural and educational institutions, including universities, colleges, and schools that draw students from across the region. These institutions add to the city's vibrant intellectual and cultural life. Additionally, Fergana is home to various cultural centers, theaters, and museums that preserve and promote the region's rich history and traditions. These institutions play a key role in preserving Fergana's cultural heritage.

Points of Interest in Fergana

Fergana offers a variety of attractions, from historical sites to cultural landmarks and natural beauty. Here are some key highlights:

Al-Fergani Park: This park, named after the medieval astronomer and mathematician Al-Fergani, is a major city attraction. Al-Fergani Park is beautifully landscaped, featuring lush greenery, walking paths, and a large statue of Al-Fergani. The park is a favorite spot for locals to relax and children to play. It often hosts cultural events and festivals, providing visitors with a glimpse into local traditions and community spirit.

Fergana Regional Museum: This museum is a must-visit for those interested in the region's history and culture. The museum houses a diverse collection of artifacts, including archaeological finds, traditional clothing, and historical documents. The exhibits offer an in-depth look at the history of Fergana and the broader Fergana Valley, from ancient times to the present. The museum also offers educational programs and temporary exhibitions, making it an engaging destination for all ages.

Fergana Bazaar: This vibrant marketplace is one of the city's most vibrant and lively places. This bustling marketplace is perfect for experiencing local culture and purchasing a variety of goods. From fresh fruits and vegetables to spices, textiles, and handmade crafts, the bazaar offers a wide range of products. The lively atmosphere and friendly vendors make it an enjoyable place to shop and explore. Visitors can also sample traditional Uzbek dishes and street food, enhancing the culinary experience.

Central Park: Central Park in Fergana is another beautiful green space that attracts both locals and tourists. The park features well-manicured lawns, flower beds, and a large fountain. It is a popular spot for families, couples, and individuals looking to enjoy a peaceful environment. The park also hosts various events, including concerts and festivals, making it a lively and dynamic place to visit.

Fergana Valley's Natural Beauty: The natural beauty of the Fergana Valley is another major attraction. Known for its fertile land, scenic landscapes, and diverse flora and fauna, the valley offers numerous opportunities for exploration and adventure. Visitors can explore the surrounding countryside, enjoy hiking and outdoor activities, and take in the stunning views of the valley. The area's natural beauty adds to Fergana's charm and provides ample opportunities for visitors to connect with nature.

Margilan City

Situated in the Fergana Valley of Uzbekistan, Margilan is a city that is celebrated for its deep cultural roots and historical importance. Primarily known for its significant role in silk production, Margilan has a rich heritage that extends over centuries. This lively city merges tradition and artistry, making it an appealing destination for travelers. Famous for its exquisite silk products, which have been valued for their quality and beauty for generations, Margilan's cultural significance is deeply intertwined with its enduring traditions of silk weaving and commerce, which continue to prosper.

Cultural Importance of Margilan

Margilan's cultural significance originates from its history as a crucial center on the Silk Road, the ancient trade route that connected the East and West. The city has been recognized for its silk production since the early medieval period. Margilan's silk products, particularly the renowned ikat fabrics, are admired for their complex designs and vibrant colors. The craft of silk weaving in Margilan has been preserved through generations, upholding traditional techniques and patterns that mirror the city's rich cultural legacy.

Silk Weaving Tradition

The tradition of silk weaving in Margilan is central to the city's identity. Silk production involves a detailed and labor-intensive process that includes raising silkworms, spinning silk threads, dyeing the fabric, and weaving intricate patterns. The ikat technique, a characteristic of Margilan's silk weaving, involves tie-dyeing the silk threads before weaving them into cloth, creating unique and colorful designs that are highly valued both locally and internationally. A visit to Margilan offers a unique opportunity to witness these traditional weaving techniques firsthand and to appreciate the skill and craftsmanship involved.

Cultural Heritage and Festivals

Margilan's cultural heritage is commemorated through various festivals and events. The city organizes several cultural festivals throughout the year, showcasing traditional music, dance, and crafts. These festivals provide a platform for local artisans to display their work and for visitors to immerse themselves in Margilan's vibrant cultural life. The festivals often feature traditional performances, craft exhibitions, and culinary delights, offering a comprehensive experience of Margilan's cultural richness.

What to See in Margilan

Margilan offers a variety of attractions that highlight its cultural and historical significance. From ancient mosques to bustling markets and traditional workshops, there are many sights to explore in this charming city. Here are some main points of interest in Margilan:

- ❖ **Yodgorlik Silk Factory:** One of Margilan's most famous attractions is the Yodgorlik Silk Factory. This factory is a living museum where visitors can observe the entire silk production process, from preparing the silk threads to the final weaving of the fabric. The Yodgorlik Silk Factory is known for its high-quality silk products, including ikat fabrics and scarves. Visitors can take guided tours of the factory, watch skilled artisans at work, and purchase beautiful silk items as souvenirs. The factory provides a fascinating insight into the traditional craft of silk weaving and its continued importance in Margilan.

- ❖ **Said Akhmad-Khoja Madrasa:** The Said Akhmad-Khoja Madrasa is a historic religious school dating back to the 19th century. This madrasa is an excellent example of Islamic architecture, featuring beautiful tile work, intricate carvings, and a serene courtyard. Although it no longer serves as an educational institution, the madrasa remains an important cultural and historical landmark in Margilan. Visitors can explore the madrasa's architecture, learn about its history, and appreciate the craftsmanship that went into its construction.

- **Margilan Bazaar:** The Margilan Bazaar is a must-visit for those looking to experience local life and buy traditional goods. This bustling market is the heart of the city's commercial activity and offers a wide range of products, from fresh produce and spices to textiles and handmade crafts. The bazaar is a vibrant place where you can experience local culture, interact with friendly vendors, and sample traditional Uzbek food. The colorful stalls and lively atmosphere make the Margilan Bazaar an enjoyable and memorable place to explore.

- **Pir Siddiq Complex:** The Pir Siddiq Complex is another important historical site in Margilan. This complex includes a mosque, a mausoleum, and a garden, and is named after Pir Siddiq, a revered Sufi saint. The complex is a place of pilgrimage for many locals and offers a peaceful environment for reflection and prayer. Visitors can explore the beautifully maintained grounds, learn about the significance of Pir Siddiq, and enjoy the tranquility of the garden.

- **Margilan History Museum:** The Margilan History Museum is dedicated to preserving and showcasing the city's rich history and cultural heritage. The museum houses a diverse collection of artifacts, including ancient coins, traditional clothing, and historical documents. The exhibits provide an in-depth look at Margilan's past, from its early days as a Silk Road trading center to its development as a major silk production hub. The museum also offers educational programs and temporary exhibitions, making it an informative and engaging destination for visitors of all ages.

Margilan's blend of historical landmarks, vibrant bazaars, and traditional workshops offers a unique glimpse into the rich cultural tapestry of Uzbekistan.

Kokand city

Situated in Uzbekistan's Fergana Valley, Kokand is a city that is celebrated for its historical and cultural richness. With its advantageous position along the historic Silk Road, Kokand has been a significant center of culture and commerce for a long time. The city's rich past is reflected in its impressive architecture, vibrant markets, and numerous landmarks that narrate the story of its dynamic history. With a population of around 200,000, Kokand offers a blend of historical allure and modern vibrancy. Visitors can explore its historical highlights and key sites, reflecting the city's enduring legacy and cultural heritage.

Historical Highlights of Kokand

Kokand's history is deeply intertwined with its role as a major hub on the Silk Road. The city has been a melting pot of various cultures, religions, and traditions, contributing to its rich historical tapestry. Here are some key historical highlights that define Kokand:

Khanate of Kokand: One of the most significant periods in Kokand's history is its era as the capital of the Khanate of Kokand. Established in the early 18th century, the khanate became a powerful state in Central Asia. Under the rule of the khans, Kokand flourished as a political, economic, and cultural center. The khanate was known for its impressive architectural achievements, many of which still stand today.

Exploring these historical sites offers a glimpse into Kokand's grandeur and sophistication during this period.

Religious and Cultural Heritage: Kokand has a rich religious and cultural heritage, with numerous mosques, madrasas (Islamic schools), and mausoleums reflecting its Islamic history. These religious sites are not only places of worship but also important cultural landmarks showcasing the city's architectural and artistic achievements. The intricate tile work, calligraphy, and decorative elements found in these buildings highlight the craftsmanship and artistry of Kokand's past.

Influence of the Silk Road: The influence of the Silk Road is evident throughout Kokand. As a major trading hub, Kokand attracted merchants, scholars, and travelers from various parts of the world. This exchange of goods, ideas, and cultures has left a lasting impact on the city. The bustling bazaars, historic caravanserais (inns for travelers), and traditional crafts reflect Kokand's role in this ancient trade network. The city's rich cultural diversity is a testament to its historical significance as a Silk Road hub.

Top Sites in Kokand

Kokand boasts a variety of attractions that showcase its historical and cultural heritage. From grand palaces to bustling markets, here are some top sites to explore in Kokand:

- **Khudayar Khan Palace:** The Khudayar Khan Palace, also known as the "Palace of the Last Khan," is one of Kokand's most impressive landmarks. Built in the mid-19th century, this grand palace was the residence of Khudayar Khan, one of the last rulers of the Khanate of Kokand. The palace features stunning architectural details, including intricate tile work, ornate ceilings, and beautiful courtyards. Visitors can explore various rooms and halls, each showcasing the opulence and grandeur of the khan's residence. The palace also houses a museum offering insight into Kokand's history and culture.

- **Jami Mosque:** The Jami Mosque is one of the largest and most important mosques in Kokand. Built in the early 19th century, this mosque is an excellent example of traditional Islamic architecture. The mosque's spacious courtyard, impressive minarets, and beautifully decorated prayer hall make it a must-visit site. The intricate woodwork and tile decorations highlight the craftsmanship and artistry of the period. The Jami Mosque continues to be an active place of worship and a significant cultural landmark in Kokand.

- **Norbutabiy Madrasah:** The Norbutabiy Madrasah is another important historical site in Kokand. This Islamic school, built in the late 18th century, served as a center of religious education and scholarship. The madrasah features a beautiful facade with intricate tile work and a spacious courtyard surrounded by classrooms and living quarters for students. Visitors can explore the madrasah and learn about its historical role in education and religious studies. The Norbutabiy Madrasah remains an important cultural and architectural landmark in Kokand.

- **Kokand Regional Studies Museum:** For those interested in the history and culture of Kokand, the Kokand Regional Studies Museum is a must-visit. The museum houses a diverse collection of artifacts, including archaeological finds, traditional clothing, and historical documents. The exhibits provide a comprehensive overview of Kokand's history, from its early days as a Silk Road trading hub to its time as the capital of the Khanate of Kokand. The museum also offers educational programs and temporary exhibitions, making it an engaging destination for visitors of all ages.

- **Dahmai Shahon Complex:** The Dahmai Shahon Complex is a significant religious and historical site in

Kokand. This complex includes several mausoleums, each housing the tombs of prominent figures from Kokand's past. The architectural style of the mausoleums reflects traditional Islamic design, with beautiful tile work and intricate carvings. The complex is a place of pilgrimage for many locals and offers a serene environment for reflection and prayer. Visitors can explore the mausoleums and learn about the historical figures buried here.

- **Kokand Bazaar:** The Kokand Bazaar is the heart of the city's commercial activity and a vibrant place to experience local culture. This bustling market offers a wide range of goods, from fresh produce and spices to textiles and handmade crafts. The bazaar is a lively and colorful place where visitors can interact with friendly vendors, sample traditional Uzbek food, and buy unique souvenirs. The Kokand Bazaar provides an authentic glimpse into the daily life and traditions of the local community

Samarkand and Dzhizak Provinces

Samarkand City

Samarkand, a city in Central Asia with a history of over 2,500 years, has been a key player in the Silk Road, the ancient trade route connecting China and the Mediterranean. Its strategic position made it a hub for various cultures, trade, religion, and intellectual exchange.

Established in the 7th century BC, Samarkand became a significant center during the Achaemenid Empire. In 329 BC, Alexander the Great took over the city, then known as Maracanda. Under the influence of Hellenistic culture, Samarkand thrived, merging Greek culture with local traditions.

The Arabs took over Samarkand in the 8th century, making it a major center of Islamic learning and culture. The Samanid dynasty further elevated its status as a leading center of Persian culture and science. However, it was during the Timurid era that Samarkand truly shone. In the 14th century, Timur (Tamerlane) declared Samarkand the capital of his vast empire, turning it into one of the world's most magnificent cities.

Under Timur and his descendants, the city witnessed the construction of grand architectural wonders, including mosques, madrasas, and mausoleums. This period saw significant advancements in astronomy, mathematics, and the arts, attracting scholars and artists from across the empire.

Samarkand's importance continued under the Shaybanid and Uzbek khanates, although its political significance declined with the rise of other regional powers. In the 19th century, it became part of the Russian Empire and later the Soviet Union, during which it underwent modern developments and preservation efforts of its historical sites. Today, Samarkand is a UNESCO World Heritage Site, recognized for its cultural and historical significance.

Key Attractions

Registan Square is the heart of Samarkand and one of the most impressive sites in Central Asia. This majestic ensemble consists of three grand madrasas: Ulugh Beg Madrasa, Sher-Dor Madrasa, and Tilya-Kori Madrasa. Built between the 15th and 17th centuries, these structures showcase stunning Islamic architecture with intricate tile work, expansive courtyards, and towering minarets.

Gur-e-Amir Mausoleum is the final resting place of Timur and a prime example of Timurid architecture. The mausoleum's ribbed azure dome and intricate tile work are breathtaking. Inside, the chamber houses the tombs of Timur, his sons, and grandsons, including Ulugh Beg. The mausoleum's design influenced later Mughal architecture in India, including the famous Taj Mahal.

Shah-i-Zinda Necropolis is a stunning complex of mausoleums and religious buildings, dating from the 11th to

19th centuries. It is renowned for its exquisite tile work and blue domes. The name Shah-i-Zinda, meaning "The Living King," refers to the mausoleum of Kusam ibn Abbas, a cousin of the Prophet Muhammad, who is believed to be buried here. The site is a pilgrimage destination, with its alleyways lined with beautifully decorated tombs of Samarkand's nobility and saints.

Bibi-Khanym Mosque, once one of the largest mosques in the Islamic world, stands as a testament to Timur's ambition. Built in the late 14th century, it was constructed to honor Timur's wife, Bibi-Khanym. The mosque's immense size and grandeur, featuring a massive entrance portal, vast courtyard, and towering domes, reflect the power and influence of Timur's empire. Although partially in ruins, the mosque remains an awe-inspiring sight.

Siab Bazaar, located next to the Bibi-Khanym Mosque, is one of Samarkand's most vibrant markets. It offers a glimpse into the daily life of locals, with stalls brimming with fresh produce, spices, nuts, sweets, and traditional crafts. The bazaar's lively atmosphere makes it a great place to experience the flavors and culture of Samarkand.

Ulugh Beg Observatory is one of Samarkand's most significant historical sites. Established in the 15th century by

Ulugh Beg, it was one of the finest observatories in the Islamic world. Ulugh Beg and his team of astronomers made remarkable contributions to astronomy, including the creation of the Zij-i-Sultani, a star catalog that remained highly accurate for centuries. The observatory's remains include a large sextant used for celestial observations.'

The Afrasiab Museum, located near the ancient site of Afrasiab (the ancient city of Samarkand), offers insights into the city's long history. The museum houses artifacts from various periods, including ceramics, coins, manuscripts, and murals. The Afrasiab murals, dating back to the 7th century, depict scenes of royal life and are among the museum's highlights.

The Tomb of the Prophet Daniel is a revered site believed to hold the remains of the biblical prophet Daniel. According to legend, Timur brought Daniel's remains to Samarkand to bring blessings to his capital. The tomb, with its unusually long sarcophagus, is a place of pilgrimage and reflects the city's spiritual heritage.

Exploring these historical and cultural landmarks in Samarkand offers a deep and enriching experience, showcasing the city's significant role in the history of Central Asia and the broader Islamic world. From its architectural marvels to its bustling bazaars, Samarkand continues to captivate visitors with its rich heritage and timeless beauty.

Dzhizak

Dzhizak, located in the heart of Uzbekistan, is a region rich in natural splendor and historical importance. It's nestled between the vast Kyzylkum Desert to the north and the towering Nuratau Mountains to the south, offering a diverse landscape that has been a strategic and cultural crossroads for centuries. The name Dzhizak, derived from Persian, means "small fort," reflecting its historical function as a defensive stronghold.

Geography and Climate

The geography of Dzhizak is diverse and impressive. The northern part of the region is covered by the Kyzylkum Desert, known for its dry climate and unique desert plants and animals. On the other hand, the southern region is marked by verdant valleys and the rugged peaks of the Nuratau Mountains. This varied landscape makes Dzhizak an attractive destination for those who love nature and adventure.

The region has a continental climate with hot summers and cold winters. The most pleasant weather for visitors is during spring and autumn, with moderate temperatures and landscapes in bloom. Rivers such as the Sanzar and Zaamin add to the scenic beauty and support local farming.

Cultural Heritage

Dzhizak has a deep cultural heritage shaped by the many civilizations that have passed through the region over thousands of years. The area has been settled since ancient times, with archaeological sites revealing traces of early communities. Historically, Dzhizak was an important stop on the Silk Road, promoting trade and cultural exchange between the East and West.

The local population is mainly Uzbek, and the region preserves strong traditional customs and practices. Visitors can experience local hospitality and cultural events, which often include traditional music, dance, and food. Dzhizak is especially known for its agricultural products, including melons, grapes, and cotton, which are celebrated during local festivals.

Notable Sites in Dzhizak

Zaamin National Park is one of Dzhizak's top attractions. Covering over 240,000 hectares, the park is a sanctuary for a wide variety of plant and animal species. Located in the western part of the Nuratau Mountains, the park offers stunning landscapes, including alpine meadows, juniper forests, and clear mountain streams. Visitors to Zaamin National Park can participate in various outdoor activities. Hiking trails of varying difficulty provide opportunities to explore the park's natural beauty. The park also contains several historical and cultural sites, such as ancient petroglyphs and the ruins of medieval settlements.

The Nurata Mountains, part of the larger Nuratau-Kyzylkum Biosphere Reserve, are known for their rugged beauty and historical significance. These mountains are decorated with petroglyphs, ancient rock carvings that provide insights into the lives of early inhabitants. The carvings depict scenes of hunting, rituals, and daily life, offering a fascinating glimpse into the past. At the foot of the mountains is the village of Nurata, home to the Chashma Complex. This site includes a sacred spring, a mosque, and the remnants of an ancient fortress believed to have been built by Alexander the Great. The holy spring is revered for its alleged healing properties, attracting many pilgrims.

Aydar Lake, also known as Aydarkul, is a large man-made lake that spans several regions, including Dzhizak. It is a scenic retreat for those looking to escape the hustle and bustle of city life. Surrounded by desert landscapes, the lake offers a striking contrast with its blue waters. Fishing is a popular activity at Aydar Lake, with abundant species such as carp and perch. The surrounding area is also ideal for camping and picnicking, providing a peaceful environment for relaxation. Birdwatchers will be particularly attracted to the lake, as it attracts a variety of migratory birds, including pelicans and flamingos.

The Kyzylkum Desert, stretching across several Central Asian countries, extends into the northern part of Dzhizak. This vast desert is characterized by its red sands, from which it gets its name ("Kyzylkum" means "Red Sands" in Turkic languages). Despite its harsh environment, the desert supports a surprising variety of life, including unique plant species and resilient wildlife. Exploring the Kyzylkum Desert offers a chance to experience the stark beauty of this arid landscape. Camel rides and off-road tours are popular ways to navigate the desert, allowing visitors to see its unique features up close. The desert is also home to traditional nomadic communities, offering a glimpse into their way of life.

Jizzakh city, the administrative center of the region, offers its own set of attractions. While it may not be as historically renowned as some other Uzbek cities, Jizzakh has several points of interest. The Jizzakh Regional Museum features exhibits on local history, culture, and the natural environment. The city's central market is a bustling hub where visitors can experience local commerce and sample regional delicacies.

CHAPTER SIX

Qashqa Darya and Surkhan Darya Provinces

Shakhrisabz

Shakhrisabz, a city in the heart of Uzbekistan, is steeped in history. Known as Kesh in the past, it's the birthplace of the famous ruler Amir Timur, also known as Tamerlane. The city's rich history is reflected in its numerous historic sites, many of which date back to the Timurid era.

Ak-Saray Palace The Ak-Saray Palace is one of Shakhrisabz's most impressive historic sites. Built by Amir Timur in the late 14th century, the palace was intended to showcase his rule's power and grandeur. Today, only the entrance gate and parts of the walls remain, but the scale and majesty of the ruins are still awe-inspiring. The gateway, which once stood 65 meters tall, is adorned with intricate tile work and inscriptions that have survived the test of time. The Ak-Saray Palace stands as a testament to Timur's ambition and the architectural prowess of his era.

Dorut Tilavat Complex The Dorut Tilavat Complex, or "the Place of Reflection," is another significant site in Shakhrisabz. This religious complex includes the Kok Gumbaz Mosque, the Gumbazi-Seyidan Mausoleum, and the Shamsiddin Kulal Mausoleum. The Kok Gumbaz Mosque, built by Timur's grandson Ulugh Beg in 1435, is notable for its impressive dome and beautiful tile work. The Gumbazi-Seyidan Mausoleum, located next to the mosque, is the final resting place of Ulugh Beg's descendants. The Shamsiddin Kulal Mausoleum is dedicated to Shamsiddin Kulal, a respected spiritual guide of Timur. The entire complex exudes a peaceful atmosphere, reflecting its role as a place of worship and contemplation.

Dor-us Siyodat Complex The Dor-us Siyodat Complex, or "Seat of Authority and Strength," is another important landmark in Shakhrisabz. This complex includes the Hazrat-i Imam Mosque and the tomb of Jahangir, Timur's eldest and most beloved son. Jahangir's tomb is particularly poignant, as Timur was said to be deeply grieved by his son's early death. The complex is known for its beautiful tile work and grand architecture, which embody the splendor of the Timurid dynasty. The Hazrat-i Imam Mosque, with its intricate designs and spiritual significance, adds to the location's historical and cultural richness.

Timur's Crypt Timur's Crypt, an underground chamber located near the Dor-us Siyodat Complex, was originally intended to be Timur's burial place. However, due to various historical events, Timur was eventually buried in Samarkand. The crypt remains an important site, offering insight into the burial practices and architectural styles of the time. The interior of the crypt is simple yet solemn, reflecting the chamber's intended purpose. Visitors can enter the crypt and contemplate the historical significance of this planned mausoleum.

Chorsu Bazaar Shakhrisabz also boasts the Chorsu Bazaar, a bustling marketplace that has been a hub of trade for centuries. The bazaar is a vibrant place where locals trade goods, from fresh fruits and spices to fabrics and crafts. The bazaar offers a glimpse into the daily life and culture of the people of Shakhrisabz. It's a great place to experience the local atmosphere, try traditional Uzbek dishes, and buy unique souvenirs. The Chorsu Bazaar is a must-visit for those looking to immerse themselves in local culture and traditions.

Karshi Karshi, a city located in the southern part of Uzbekistan, is an intriguing place that blends history, tradition, and modernity. As the administrative center of the Qashqadaryo Region, Karshi has a deep-rooted heritage that dates back to ancient times. Its strategic location on the historic Silk Road has contributed to its diverse cultural blend. Here, we highlight the main attractions and local insights that make Karshi a destination worth visiting.

Main Attractions Odina Mosque The Odina Mosque is one of Karshi's most important historical sites. This grand mosque, built in the 16th century, served as a significant religious and educational center. The mosque's design showcases the exceptional craftsmanship of the era, with detailed tile work and elegantly designed minarets. While parts of the mosque have been affected by time, ongoing restoration projects aim to preserve its historical and cultural value. Visitors can appreciate the intricate artistry and experience the peaceful ambiance of this respected place of worship.

Khoja Saroy Madrasa The Khoja Saroy Madrasa, an educational institution from the 17th century, is a testament to the city's rich intellectual heritage. The building's design is a prime example of the Islamic style common in Central Asia, featuring a courtyard surrounded by study rooms and decorated with elaborate ornaments. Today, the madrasa functions as a museum, providing insights into the region's educational and religious past. A visit to the madrasa offers a look into the academic pursuits and daily routines of those who once studied there.

Caravanserais Due to its strategic position on the Silk Road, Karshi has historically been an important stop for traders and travelers. The city was home to several caravanserais, which served as rest stops for merchants and their caravans. While many of these structures have not survived the passage of time, the remnants of a few still stand, offering a glimpse into the city's vibrant past. These caravanserais played a crucial role in the exchange of goods and ideas, contributing to the cultural and economic dynamism of Karshi. Visitors can explore these historical sites and envision the bustling trade activities that once occurred within their walls.

Karshi Fort The Karshi Fort, another historical site, dates back to the medieval period. The fort was instrumental in protecting the city from invasions and functioned as a military stronghold. Although much of the fort is in ruins, the remaining structures provide a sense of the formidable defenses that once protected the city. The fort's strategic location offers panoramic views of the surrounding landscape, making it a popular spot for history buffs and photographers alike. A visit to the fort allows visitors to delve into the military history of Karshi and appreciate the architectural ingenuity of its builders.

The Green Market No trip to Karshi is complete without a visit to the Green Market, the city's lively central bazaar. This bustling market offers a sensory feast with its variety of fresh produce, spices, textiles, and traditional handicrafts. The market is a great place to experience the local culture and interact with friendly vendors. Sampling local delicacies, such as plov (a savory rice dish), samsa (savory pastries), and various sweets, is a must. The Green Market not only provides a shopping experience but also serves as a cultural hub where the city's residents gather and socialize.

Boysun

Boysun, a quaint town in the southeast of Uzbekistan, is a place where culture and nature come together. It's located at the base of the Gissar Range, and it's a place where visitors can experience Uzbek traditions and enjoy beautiful scenery. Boysun has a lot to offer, from ancient sites to lively markets.

Boysun Mountains The mountains surrounding Boysun are a sight to behold and offer many outdoor activities. There are hiking trails for all skill levels, leading to amazing views, secluded valleys, and waterfalls. The mountains are rich in plant and animal life, making them a dream for nature enthusiasts and photographers.

Teshik-Tash Cave This cave is a significant archaeological site in the region. It became famous when a Neanderthal child's remains, estimated to be around 70,000 years old, were found here. The cave offers a look into the area's prehistoric inhabitants. Visitors can explore the cave and learn about the early human settlements in this part of Uzbekistan.

Local Markets The markets in Boysun are full of life, with locals buying and selling a range of goods. You can find fresh produce, spices, textiles, and handicrafts. Visiting a market is a great way to see the daily life of the people in Boysun. The markets are also a good place to buy souvenirs and gifts, like traditional embroidered textiles and pottery.

Boysun Bahori Festival One of the highlights of Boysun is the Boysun Bahori Festival, which marks the start of spring. This festival, recognized by UNESCO as part of the Intangible Cultural Heritage of Humanity, showcases the town's cultural traditions. During the festival, visitors can enjoy traditional music and dance, handicraft exhibitions, and local food.

Historic Sites Boysun has several historic sites that take you back in time. The remains of ancient fortresses and caravanserais show Boysun's importance on historic trade routes. These structures, though worn by time, still show their past grandeur. The Sayyid Ali Akbar Mausoleum, dedicated to a well-known Sufi saint, is a peaceful and historically significant site worth visiting.

Traditional Villages The villages around Boysun are just as charming, each with its own cultural practices. Visiting these villages lets travelers see rural life in Uzbekistan and traditional farming methods, crafts, and community activities. The villagers' hospitality often means that visitors are welcomed into homes, offering a deeper understanding of the local lifestyle.

Local Cuisine Boysun's cuisine reflects its cultural heritage. Traditional dishes are made with locally sourced ingredients. Plov (a rice dish with meat and vegetables), shashlik (grilled meat skewers), and manti (dumplings) are popular dishes. The town is also known for its dairy products, like kurt (dried yogurt balls) and qatiq (fermented milk). Eating a meal with a local family is a great way to experience Boysun's food traditions.

Music and Dance Performances Music and dance are important parts of Boysun's culture. The town has a variety of traditional musical instruments, like the doira (a drum) and the dutar (a two-stringed lute). Local musicians often perform folk songs about love, bravery, and daily life. Traditional dances, with their elegant movements and colorful costumes, are also a highlight.

Shrines and Mausoleums Boysun has several shrines and mausoleums that are important for religious and historical reasons. These sites are often visited by locals who come to pay their respects and seek blessings. The Sayyid Ali Akbar Mausoleum, dedicated to a prominent Sufi saint, is a revered site. The beautiful architecture and peaceful atmosphere of these shrines offer a quiet retreat for visitors.

Denau

Denau, a gem nestled in southern Uzbekistan, throws open its arms to visitors seeking a unique blend of historical wonders, vibrant culture, and breathtaking natural beauty. Sitting close to the Tajik border, Denau offers an off-the-beaten-path adventure for those who prefer to explore hidden treasures.

1. Sayyid Ata Mausoleum: One of Denau's most significant landmarks is the Sayyid Ata Mausoleum. This revered structure honors Sayyid Ata, a Sufi saint who played a pivotal role in spreading Islam throughout the region. The mausoleum itself exemplifies Islamic architectural mastery, adorned with intricate tilework, calligraphy, and a peaceful courtyard. Visitors can wander the tranquil grounds, gaining insights into Denau's rich spiritual tapestry. This site transcends its role as a place of worship, standing as a historical monument that reflects the town's deep-rooted religious traditions.

2. Kokildor-Ota Mosque: Another crucial religious site in Denau is the Kokildor-Ota Mosque, renowned for its captivating architecture and serene atmosphere. The mosque boasts elegant minarets, a spacious prayer hall, and beautifully decorated interiors. It serves as a focal point for community gatherings and religious practices. A visit allows travelers to appreciate the architectural marvel and gain understanding of Islam's influence on the daily lives of Denau's residents. The Kokildor-Ota Mosque stands as a powerful symbol of the town's enduring cultural and religious heritage.

3. Denau Bazaar: No Denau experience is complete without losing yourself in the bustling Denau Bazaar. This vibrant marketplace pulsates with energy as locals come together to trade a dazzling array of goods. From the freshest produce and aromatic spices to colorful textiles and everyday necessities, the bazaar is a feast for the senses. As you wander through the maze of stalls, soak up the lively atmosphere and witness the trading practices that have been embedded in Denau's culture for centuries. This is an excellent spot to pick up unique souvenirs, such as handcrafted items and local delicacies, offering a taste of Denau's daily life.

4. Unveiling the Past: Denau boasts a treasure trove of archaeological sites that provide a window into the region's ancient past. These sites encompass remnants of bygone settlements and fortresses, dating back to the pre-Islamic era. Exploring these hidden gems allows visitors to grasp the historical significance of Denau and its strategic position along historical trade routes. Guided tours are often available, shedding light on the fascinating history and discoveries made at these locations. Denau's archaeological sites serve as undeniable proof of the town's rich and multifaceted heritage.

5. Local Museums: Denau's local museums offer a captivating journey through the region's history, culture, and artistic expressions. These museums showcase a diverse range of exhibits, including archaeological artifacts, traditional garments, and historical documents. The Denau Regional Museum is a must-see for those curious about the town's past, offering a comprehensive exploration of Denau's journey from ancient times to the present day.

Visiting these museums provides valuable context and enriches the overall experience of exploring Denau. They act as educational resources, highlighting the town's significant cultural and historical contributions.

6. Kyzyl-Kala Fortress: Standing guard near Denau is the Kyzyl-Kala Fortress, an ancient fortification. With its imposing walls and strategic location, this fortress played a critical role in safeguarding the region from invasions. The site offers breathtaking views of the surrounding landscape and provides insights into the area's military history. Visitors can explore the ruins of the fortress, using their imagination to recreate the historical events that unfolded within its walls. The Kyzyl-Kala Fortress stands as an impressive historical landmark, reflecting Denau's significant role in regional defense and trade.

7. Nature's Paradise: Denau is embraced by captivating natural landscapes, perfect for outdoor enthusiasts. Nature reserves in the vicinity offer opportunities for hiking, bird watching, and immersing yourself in the serene environment. These reserves are home to a diverse array of plant and animal life, making them ideal destinations for nature lovers. The scenic beauty of the area provides a refreshing contrast to the town's historical sites and bustling markets. Exploring the nature reserves surrounding Denau allows visitors to experience the region's natural wonders and find tranquility.

Termez

Historical Overview Termez, situated in the southern part of Uzbekistan near Afghanistan's border, is among the oldest cities in the country. With a history spanning over 2,500 years, Termez holds immense historical value. The city has been a convergence point for various cultures and civilizations, shaped by different empires and religions over its extensive history. Initially established by the ancient Bactrians, Termez later evolved into a significant center during the Kushan Empire, a dominant entity in Central Asia around the 1st century AD. The city prospered as a center of Buddhism, with numerous monasteries and stupas constructed here. This era witnessed the establishment of important religious and educational institutions that drew scholars and pilgrims from all over the region. With the Islamic conquest in the 7th and 8th centuries, Termez transformed into an Islamic city and continued to prosper under various dynasties, including the Samanids, Ghaznavids, and Timurids. Each of these eras contributed to the city's cultural and architectural landscape. The city was a significant hub of trade, learning, and religious activity, as evidenced by the many mosques, madrasas, and mausoleums scattered throughout the area. In the 13th century, Termez suffered extensive damage due to the Mongol invasions led by Genghis Khan. However, it was reconstructed and managed to reclaim some of its former prominence in the subsequent centuries. The city's strategic location on the banks of the Amu Darya River and its position along the Silk Road ensured its continued importance as a commercial and cultural intersection. Today, Termez is a lively city that offers visitors an intriguing look into its rich and diverse past. Its historical sites and monuments stand as a testament to the city's enduring significance over thousands of years.

Tourist Attractions

Al-Hakim at-Termezi Mausoleum

The Al-Hakim at-Termezi Mausoleum is one of Termez's most important historical and religious landmarks. It is dedicated to Al-Hakim at-Termezi, a famous Sufi scholar and mystic who lived in the 9th century. The mausoleum complex includes the scholar's tomb, a mosque, and a garden. The architecture of the mausoleum beautifully combines Islamic design and local craftsmanship, featuring detailed tile work, calligraphy, and tranquil courtyards. Visitors can learn about the life and teachings of Al-Hakim at-Termezi while enjoying the peaceful ambiance of the site.

Sultan Saodat Ensemble

The Sultan Saodat Ensemble is a remarkable architectural complex that dates back to the 10th century. It served as the burial site for the Sayyid dynasty, descendants of the Prophet Muhammad. The ensemble consists of several mausoleums, mosques, and madrasas, showcasing a variety of architectural styles and decorative techniques. The complex is known for its beautiful brickwork, domes, and arches. Exploring the Sultan Saodat Ensemble allows visitors to learn about the rich history of the Sayyid dynasty and appreciate the artistic achievements of the period.

Fayaz-Tepa

Fayaz-Tepa is an ancient Buddhist monastery complex located near Termez. Dating back to the 2nd century AD, it is one of the most significant remnants of Buddhism in Central Asia. The site includes a well-preserved stupa, monastic cells, and various artifacts that provide insight into the Buddhist practices and way of life during that era. Fayaz-Tepa offers a unique opportunity to explore the Buddhist heritage of Termez and understand the city's role as a major center of Buddhism in ancient times.

Kara-Tepe

Kara-Tepe is another significant archaeological site that highlights the Buddhist past of Termez. This complex of cave monasteries and temples was carved into a hillside and used by monks for meditation and religious rituals. The site dates back to the 1st to 4th centuries AD and contains numerous statues, murals, and inscriptions. Kara-Tepe provides an intriguing look into the early Buddhist architecture and art of the region. Walking through the cave temples, visitors can imagine the spiritual devotion and daily activities of the ancient monks who once inhabited this site.

Zurmala Tower

The Zurmala Tower is a striking architectural remnant of a Buddhist stupa that dates back to the 3rd century AD. This towering structure, standing at about 12 meters high, was part of a larger Buddhist complex that once existed in Termez. The tower is notable for its impressive height and cylindrical shape, making it a prominent landmark in the area. Although much of the original structure has not survived, the Zurmala Tower remains an important symbol of Termez's Buddhist heritage

Termez Archaeological Museum

For those with a keen interest in the region's rich past, the Termez Archaeological Museum is a place not to be missed. The museum is home to a wide array of artifacts from different eras, including the ancient Bactrian, Kushan, and Islamic periods. The exhibits, which include pottery, coins, sculptures, and manuscripts, offer a thorough understanding of Termez's historical and cultural evolution. The museum provides essential context for comprehending the city's archaeological sites and the varied influences that have shaped its history.

Minaret of Jarkurgan

Situated a short distance from Termez, the Jarkurgan Minaret is a remarkable 12th-century structure that displays the architectural prowess of the Karakhanid dynasty. The minaret, standing at 21 meters, is decorated with detailed brickwork and ornamental patterns. Initially part of a larger mosque complex, the Jarkurgan Minaret is one of the few remaining examples of Karakhanid architecture in the region. A visit to the minaret offers insight into the architectural styles and religious structures of the period.

Bridge of Friendship

The Bridge of Friendship, which crosses the Amu Darya River, serves as a connection between Uzbekistan and Afghanistan. While it is primarily a functional structure, it also holds symbolic importance as a link between two countries with deep historical and cultural connections. The bridge provides picturesque views of the river and the surrounding landscape, making it a significant landmark in Termez. Visitors can appreciate the strategic importance of this crossing point and its role in promoting trade and communication between the two countries.

Fortress of Kampyr-Tepe

Kampyr-Tepe is an ancient fortress site that harks back to the Hellenistic period. It was initially established by the successors of Alexander the Great and later expanded during the Kushan Empire. The site includes the remains of defensive walls, towers, and residential structures, offering insight into the military and urban planning of the time. Kampyr-Tepe is an intriguing archaeological site that underscores the historical importance of Termez as a strategic stronghold

CHAPTER SEVEN

Navoi Provinced

Navoi Navoi, nestled in the core of Uzbekistan, is a relatively new city with a deep historical context and a contemporary industrial profile. The city, established in 1958 during the Soviet period, is named after the esteemed Uzbek poet Alisher Navoi. Despite its recent inception, the region surrounding Navoi has a history that spans thousands of years. The region around Navoi has been populated since the olden times. It was a part of the grand Silk Road, the ancient trade route that linked the East and West. The Silk Road not only facilitated trade but also cultural exchange, and the region of Navoi became a convergence point for diverse cultures and civilizations. Over the centuries, this region has been under the rule of various empires and dynasties, including the Achaemenids, the Sassanids, and the Timurids, each leaving behind a legacy of rich historical and cultural landmarks. During the Soviet era, Navoi was developed into an industrial center. The Soviet government set up several large industrial complexes in the city, including chemical plants, mining operations, and manufacturing facilities. This industrial surge played a pivotal role in the economic development of Uzbekistan, and Navoi emerged as one of the key centers of Soviet industrialization in Central Asia. Today, Navoi continues to be a significant industrial city in Uzbekistan, recognized for its substantial contributions to the country's economy. However, it's not just its industrial strength that makes Navoi noteworthy. The city and its surroundings are home to several historical and cultural attractions that offer a glimpse into the rich heritage of the region.

Tourist Attractions

Navoi Theater

The Navoi Theater, named in honor of the celebrated poet Alisher Navoi, is a cultural landmark in the city. It serves as a center for performing arts, hosting a variety of cultural events, including opera, ballet, and theatrical performances. The theater's architecture is an impressive mix of traditional Uzbek and modern Soviet styles, featuring intricate decorations and a grand auditorium. Attending a performance at the Navoi Theater offers a unique cultural experience and a chance to appreciate the artistic heritage of Uzbekistan.

Rabati Malik Caravanserai

Rabati Malik Caravanserai Situated on the outskirts of Navoi, the Rabati Malik Caravanserai is a historical site that dates back to the 11th century. This ancient inn was constructed to provide shelter and rest to travelers along the Silk Road. The caravanserai is an excellent example of Islamic architecture, with its grand entrance, arched hallways, and spacious courtyards. Although partially in ruins, the site still exudes a sense of historical grandeur. Visitors can explore the remains of this ancient inn and imagine the bustling activity of merchants and travelers that once passed through its gates.

Sarmishsay Petroglyphs

The Sarmishsay Gorge, located near Navoi, is home to one of the largest collections of petroglyphs in Central Asia. These ancient rock carvings date back to the Bronze Age and provide a fascinating glimpse into the lives and beliefs of early inhabitants of the region. The petroglyphs depict scenes of hunting, rituals, and everyday life, offering valuable insights into the culture and traditions of ancient communities. The gorge is also a beautiful natural site, with stunning landscapes and diverse flora and fauna. A visit to Sarmishsay is both an archaeological and natural adventure.

Aidarkul Lake

Aidarkul Lake is a large, artificial lake located near Navoi. It was created in the 1960s as a result of Soviet irrigation projects. Today, the lake is a popular destination for recreation and relaxation. The serene waters of Aidarkul are ideal for swimming, fishing, and boating. The surrounding area is a haven for birdwatchers, with many species of migratory birds making a stop at the lake. The tranquil environment and beautiful scenery make Aidarkul Lake a perfect spot for a day trip from Navoi.

Nurata Mountains and Chashma Complex

The Nurata Mountains, located to the north of Navoi, offer a stunning natural backdrop and a wealth of historical sites. One of the most notable attractions in this area is the Chashma Complex in the town of Nurata. The complex is centered around a holy spring, which, according to local legend, was created by a strike from the staff of the prophet Moses. The water of the spring is believed to have healing properties, and it attracts pilgrims from all over Uzbekistan. The Chashma Complex includes a mosque, a medieval fortress, and ancient petroglyphs. The area is also known for its beautiful landscapes, with opportunities for hiking and exploring the scenic mountains.

Fayzabad Complex

The Fayzabad Complex is a historical and religious site located in the vicinity of Navoi. It comprises a mausoleum, a mosque, and a madrasa, all built during the 16th century. The complex is named after Sheikh Khodja Fayzabad, a prominent religious figure of the time. The architecture of the complex is a fine example of Timurid design, featuring elaborate tile work and beautiful geometric patterns. The Fayzabad Complex is not only a place of worship but also a symbol of the rich Islamic heritage of the region.

Uchkuduk Uchkuduk

Uchkuduk Uchkuduk, meaning "Three Wells," is a small town near Navoi that gained fame due to the popular Soviet song "Uchkuduk, Three Wells." The town is situated in the Kyzylkum Desert and is known for its uranium mining operations. While primarily an industrial town, Uchkuduk offers a glimpse into the life of a desert community and the challenges of mining in such a harsh environment. Visitors interested in industrial history and desert landscapes may find Uchkuduk an intriguing place to visit.

Kyzylkum Desert

The vast Kyzylkum Desert surrounds Navoi, offering a stark but beautiful landscape of sand dunes, scrubland, and rugged terrain. The desert is a haven for adventure enthusiasts, with opportunities for camel trekking, off-road driving, and camping under the starry sky. The Kyzylkum Desert is also home to unique wildlife, including the endangered Saiga antelope. Exploring the desert provides a sense of the vastness and beauty of Uzbekistan's natural environment.

Karmana

Karmana, a town of historical significance nestled in the Navoi region of Uzbekistan, is a place where history and culture intertwine. The town's roots trace back to ancient times, and it has been a meeting point for various civilizations, each leaving its imprint on Karmana.

The Sheikh Nuriddin Complex

The Sheikh Nuriddin Complex, one of the most notable historical sites in Karmana, is a religious and educational complex dedicated to Sheikh Nuriddin, a respected Islamic scholar and mystic. The complex encompasses a mosque, a mausoleum, and a madrasa (Islamic school). The architecture of the Sheikh Nuriddin Complex is a prime example of Islamic design, featuring detailed tile work, graceful arches, and beautifully adorned interiors. Visitors can explore the tranquil courtyards, the prayer halls, and the mausoleum, which is a pilgrimage site for many devout Muslims.

The Oq Gumbaz Mosque

The Oq Gumbaz Mosque, also known as the White Dome Mosque, is another significant historical site in Karmana. This mosque is famous for its striking white dome and its architectural elegance. Constructed during the Timurid era, the Oq Gumbaz Mosque displays the magnificence of Islamic architecture with its large domed structure, intricate mosaics, and finely carved decorations. The mosque has been well-preserved and continues to be a place of worship and a testament to the town's historical importance.

Ancient Caravanserai Karmana

The Ancient Caravanserai Karmana was once a crucial stop along the Silk Road, and evidence of its historical importance as a trade hub can still be seen today. The town houses the remains of an ancient caravanserai, a type of inn where merchants and travelers could rest and resupply. The caravanserai in Karmana is an intriguing site to explore, offering a glimpse into the town's vibrant past as a center of commerce and cultural exchange. The structure, although partially in ruins, retains its historical charm and gives visitors a sense of the bustling activity that once took place within its walls.

The Khisrav Madrasa

The Khisrav Madrasa is another significant historical site in Karmana. This Islamic educational institution was constructed during the 16th century and served as a center for religious learning. The madrasa features traditional Islamic architecture, with a grand entrance, spacious courtyards, and intricately designed lecture halls. The Khisrav Madrasa has played a significant role in the town's history, nurturing generations of scholars and contributing to the spread of Islamic knowledge and culture in the region.

Sightseeing Spots

Sightseeing Spots In addition to its historical sites, Karmana offers several other attractions that make it a worthwhile destination for travelers interested in exploring the cultural and natural beauty of Uzbekistan.

Karmana Market

The bustling Karmana Market is a vibrant place where visitors can experience the local culture and lifestyle. The market is filled with colorful stalls selling a variety of goods, including fresh produce, spices, textiles, and traditional handicrafts. It is an excellent place to shop for souvenirs, sample local delicacies, and interact with the friendly residents of Karmana. The lively atmosphere of the market provides a unique insight into the daily life of the town's inhabitants.

The Karmana Cultural Center

The Karmana Cultural Center is a hub for local arts and culture. The center hosts various cultural events, including music performances, dance shows, and art exhibitions. It is a great place to learn about the rich cultural heritage of Karmana and to experience traditional Uzbek music and dance. The cultural center also offers workshops and classes on traditional crafts, providing visitors with an opportunity to engage with the local culture in a meaningful way.

Nurata Mountains

The nearby Nurata Mountains offer stunning natural beauty and a range of outdoor activities for nature enthusiasts. The mountains are known for their scenic landscapes, with rolling hills, lush valleys, and picturesque villages. Visitors can enjoy hiking, trekking, and birdwatching in this pristine natural environment. The Nurata Mountains are also home to several historical and archaeological sites, including ancient petroglyphs and ruins, making it a perfect destination for those interested in both nature and history.

Local Crafts Workshops

Local Crafts Workshops Karmana is known for its traditional crafts, and visitors have the opportunity to participate in workshops and learn about the town's artisanal heritage. Local craftsmen offer workshops on pottery, weaving, and embroidery, allowing visitors to create their own handmade souvenirs. These workshops provide a hands-on experience and a deeper appreciation for the skill and artistry involved in traditional Uzbek crafts. It is also a great way to support local artisans and preserve the town's cultural heritage.

Bukhara Province
Bukhara and Gijduvan

Bukhara and Gijduvan, two notable cities in Uzbekistan, are celebrated for their deep historical roots and cultural richness. Bukhara, one of Central Asia's oldest cities, has been a significant hub of commerce, culture, and religion for many centuries. Its well-maintained medieval architecture and monuments make it an intriguing destination for those interested in history. Gijduvan, situated just 50 kilometers from Bukhara, is recognized for its traditional pottery and crafts. Together, these cities offer a wealth of must-see sites that provide a profound insight into Uzbekistan's illustrious past and vibrant traditions.

Must-See Sites in Bukhara

Ark Fortress

The Ark Fortress, an ancient stronghold in Bukhara, stands as a symbol of the city's extensive and eventful history. Constructed around the 5th century AD, the fortress was the dwelling of Bukhara's rulers for many centuries. Visitors can explore its various sections, including the throne room, reception halls, and courtyards. The fortress also houses a museum that displays artifacts from different periods of Bukhara's history, including coins, manuscripts, and weapons. The Ark's imposing walls and remarkable architecture provide a glimpse into the city's defensive capabilities and its significance as a political and military center.

Bolo Haouz Mosque

The Bolo Haouz Mosque, situated near the Ark Fortress, is one of Bukhara's most stunning mosques. Constructed in the early 18th century, the mosque features a captivating facade with intricately carved wooden pillars and a breathtaking ceiling adorned with colorful geometric patterns. The mosque's name, which translates to "mosque near the pool," refers to the picturesque pool in front of it. The serene atmosphere and architectural beauty of the Bolo Haouz Mosque make it a must-see site for those interested in Islamic architecture and history.

Poi Kalyan Complex

The Poi Kalyan Complex is one of Bukhara's most iconic landmarks. This grand complex includes the Kalyan Minaret, the Kalyan Mosque, and the Mir-i-Arab Madrasa. The Kalyan Minaret, also known as the "Tower of Death," was built in the 12th century and is one of the tallest minarets in Central Asia. The Kalyan Mosque, with its vast courtyard and majestic dome, is a masterpiece of Islamic architecture. The Mir-i-Arab Madrasa, an important center of religious education, features beautiful tile work and intricate decorations. Together, these structures form a stunning ensemble that reflects the architectural and cultural achievements of Bukhara.

Lyab-i Hauz Ensemble

The Lyab-i Hauz Ensemble is a picturesque plaza in the heart of Bukhara, surrounded by historic buildings and centered around a tranquil pool. This ensemble includes the Nadir Divan-Begi Khanaka, the Nadir Divan-Begi Madrasa, and the Kukeldash Madrasa. The Nadir Divan-Begi Madrasa, originally built as a caravanserai, features stunning mosaics and decorative tile work. The Kukeldash Madrasa is one of the largest madrasas in Bukhara and boasts impressive architectural details. The Lyab-i Hauz Ensemble is a popular gathering place for locals and visitors alike, offering a peaceful atmosphere and a glimpse into the city's vibrant social life.

Samanid Mausoleum

The Samanid Mausoleum, dating back to the 9th century, is one of the oldest and most well-preserved monuments in Bukhara. This mausoleum, built to honor the founder of the Samanid dynasty, Ismail Samani, is an architectural gem with its intricate brickwork and geometric designs. The structure's unique design, featuring a square base and a domed roof, is considered a masterpiece of early Islamic architecture. Visiting the Samanid Mausoleum provides a fascinating insight into the artistic and architectural achievements of the Samanid period.

Must-See Sites in Gijduvan

Gijduvan Pottery Workshop

Gijduvan is famous for its traditional pottery, and visiting a pottery workshop is a must. The town's pottery tradition dates back over a thousand years, and its artisans are known for their skill and creativity. The Gijduvan Pottery Workshop offers visitors a chance to see master potters at work, creating beautiful ceramics using traditional techniques. The workshop also has a gallery where you can purchase unique handcrafted items, such as plates, bowls, and vases. The vibrant colors and intricate patterns of Gijduvan pottery make these items highly prized souvenirs.

Abd al-Khalik Gijduvani Memorial Complex

The Abd al-Khalik Gijduvani Memorial Complex is dedicated to one of the most revered Sufi scholars and spiritual leaders in Central Asia, Abd al-Khalik Gijduvani. This complex includes a mosque, a mausoleum, and a madrasah. The site is an important pilgrimage destination for Sufi followers and a place of spiritual significance. Visitors can explore the beautifully decorated mausoleum and learn about the teachings and life of Abd al-Khalik Gijduvani. The peaceful atmosphere and spiritual ambiance of the complex make it a significant cultural and religious site in Gijduvan.

Gijduvan Market

The Gijduvan Market is a bustling place where you can experience the local culture and buy traditional goods. The market offers a wide variety of products, including fresh produce, spices, textiles, and handmade crafts. It's a great place to interact with local vendors, sample traditional Uzbek foods, and buy unique souvenirs. The lively atmosphere and diverse array of goods make the Gijduvan Market a must-visit site for anyone wanting to experience the local way of life.

Juma Mosque

The Juma Mosque in Gijduvan is an important religious site and a beautiful example of Islamic architecture. This mosque, with its elegant minarets and spacious courtyard, serves as a central place of worship for the local community. The mosque's interior is adorned with intricate tile work and calligraphy, reflecting the artistic heritage of the region. Visiting the Juma Mosque provides an opportunity to appreciate the architectural beauty and religious significance of this historic site.

Khorezm Province
Urgench and Khiva

These two cities in Uzbekistan, are known for their rich historical and cultural legacy. Situated in the Khorezm region, these cities offer a captivating journey through history, showcasing architectural wonders and historical landmarks that provide a deep understanding of Uzbekistan's illustrious past. Khiva, with its well-preserved ancient town, is particularly famous for its historical monuments and stunning Islamic architecture. Urgench, acting as a gateway to Khiva, also has its own unique attractions. Together, these cities offer a range of must-see sites that capture the imagination and highlight the region's historical importance.

Must-See Sites in Khiva

Itchan Kala

At the heart of Khiva lies Itchan Kala, the inner city enclosed by walls, which is a UNESCO World Heritage site. Itchan Kala is an open-air museum filled with over 50 historical monuments and 250 old houses, reflecting the city's rich architectural heritage. The city walls, constructed of mud bricks and standing 10 meters high, surround the old town, creating a distinct sense of stepping back in time.

Key highlights within Itchan Kala include

- **Kunya-Ark Fortress:** Constructed in the 17th century, this fortress was the dwelling of Khiva's rulers. Visitors

can explore various sections of the fortress, including the throne room, the mint, the harem, and the mosque. The fortress also offers a panoramic view of the city from its ramparts.
- **Muhammad Amin Khan Madrasa:** This madrasa, one of the largest in Central Asia, was built in 1851 and features a large courtyard surrounded by two-story arcades. It now houses a hotel, allowing visitors to experience the historic ambiance firsthand.
- **Juma Mosque:** Known for its 213 wooden pillars, some dating back to the 10th century, the Juma Mosque is an architectural marvel. The pillars, carved with intricate designs, support a flat roof, creating a unique and serene interior space.

Kalta Minor Minaret

The Kalta Minor Minaret is one of Khiva's most iconic landmarks. This unfinished minaret, intended to be the tallest in the Islamic world, stands at 29 meters high. Despite its incomplete state, the minaret is striking due to its turquoise-tiled facade. The vibrant tiles catch the sunlight, making the minaret a standout feature of Khiva's skyline.

Tash Hauli Palace

The Tash Hauli Palace, built in the 19th century, was the residence of the Khiva khans and their families. The palace complex includes the harem, the courtroom, and the reception hall. The walls and ceilings are adorned with intricate tile work and carved wooden decorations. The harem, in particular, is noted for its colorful and elaborate decor, reflecting the opulence of the era.

Pakhlavan Mahmoud Mausoleum

The Pakhlavan Mahmoud Mausoleum is dedicated to the poet, philosopher, and wrestler Pakhlavan Mahmoud, who is considered a patron saint of Khiva. The mausoleum, with its turquoise dome and richly decorated interior, is a significant religious site. The tomb itself is adorned with beautiful tile work, and the complex includes a mosque and a courtyard, providing a peaceful place for reflection and prayer.

Islam Khodja Minaret and Madrasa

The Islam Khodja Minaret, completed in 1910, is the tallest structure in Khiva, standing at 57 meters. Its slender, tapering design is complemented by bands of blue and white tiles. Visitors can climb the minaret for a breathtaking view of the city. Adjacent to the minaret is the Islam Khodja Madrasa, which features a museum displaying a collection of traditional Uzbek crafts and artifacts.

Places to Visit in Urgench

While Urgench may be less known compared to its neighbor Khiva, it has its own unique attractions that are worth a visit. As the administrative hub of the Khorezm region, Urgench provides a snapshot of modern Uzbek life while maintaining a connection to its historical roots.

Urgench Market

The Urgench Market is a lively marketplace where locals gather to trade a wide range of goods. From fresh fruits and vegetables to spices, textiles, and household items, the market offers a colorful glimpse into everyday life in Urgench. Visitors can immerse themselves in the vibrant atmosphere, taste local foods, and buy distinctive souvenirs.

Central Park and Al-Khorezmi Monument

Central Park in Urgench is a welcoming green space where locals come to relax and socialize. The park also features the Al-Khorezmi Monument, dedicated to the renowned mathematician and scholar Al-Khorezmi, who is recognized as the pioneer of algebra. The monument and the park surrounding it provide a tranquil setting for a leisurely walk.

Museum of History and Regional Traditions

The Museum of History and Regional Traditions in Urgench provides an enlightening exploration into the history and culture of the Khorezm region. The museum's exhibits span various eras, from ancient times to the present, and feature artifacts such as age-old tools, pottery, manuscripts, and traditional attire. The museum offers a thorough understanding of the region's rich heritage.

CONCLUSION

As we wrap up this travel guide, it's crucial to remember that Uzbekistan is more than just a destination; it's a journey into the heart of Central Asia. It's a place where history isn't just confined to museums but is a part of everyday life. The stories of conquerors and scholars, the craftsmanship of artisans, and the traditions of its hospitable people all weave together to form a unique Uzbek tapestry. Whether you're a history buff, a culture enthusiast, or a nature explorer, Uzbekistan has something special for every traveler. It's a land where every nook and cranny holds a new discovery, and every experience leaves an indelible impression. As you reflect on the journey through this guide, may it inspire you to explore Uzbekistan firsthand, to tread its ancient paths, to relish its culinary delights, and to connect with its warm-hearted people. In the end, Uzbekistan is more than just a point on a map—it's a destination that touches the heart and soul. It reminds us that travel isn't just about visiting new places but about understanding diverse cultures, embracing fresh perspectives, and finding beauty in our shared human experience. As you set off on your travels, may the timeless tapestry of Uzbekistan remain with you, a treasured memory of a land where history and hospitality are intertwined.

Printed in Great Britain
by Amazon

45256707R00089